Career with Purpose
A Guide to Finding the Work You Love

by

Michael Grubich and Mike Milsted

Advance Praise

"*Career with Purpose* is more of a career mentor than a book. Grubich and Milsted pack every chapter with tips, techniques, and inspirational stories from brand-building, to controlling the interview process, to negotiating with confidence, to excelling in your first 90 days. This book will be a life-long resource guide."

Tammy McCormack
Chief Human Resource Officer
Nassco, Inc.

"So many of us are wandering the work world with no chosen destination. How can you chart a course for career happiness if you don't know where you're going? *Career with Purpose* will help you find that place and tell you how to get there."

Vince Vitrano
Emmy Award–winning American journalist and anchor

"Having purpose, working at what makes you happy, and working with others who share your values and interests satisfy the basic needs for a fulfilling career. You'll find yourself and your voice in these valuable pages."

Dayla Randolph, PhD
Chief Talent Officer
Advocate Aurora Health

"This is all about you and what you want out of your work life! This book is your travel guide as you career with purpose. Know your story, build a brand around it, and work at what you love with Grubich and Milsted's captivating assistance and provocative thoughts."

Flavia Ziarnik
Global Strategic Sourcing Manager
Generac Power Systems

"*Career with Purpose* is the ultimate job searcher's guide. Grubich and Milsted go beyond theory and pack each chapter with insights, best methods, and motivating stories that help the reader navigate their career and discover greater work satisfaction."

Matthew Moulton

Executive Advisor, Consultant & Business Coach

"Simply thinking of 'career' as a verb, rather than a noun, is a game changer. Find a way to align your passion and motivation with your daily work—then you have found happiness. Work with purpose."

Elizabeth Borgen D.B.A.

President

Lakeland University

"Grubich and Milsted's approach to understanding who and where you are in your work life story and career is enlightening. The book is reflective, insightful, and a master class for truly creating your own next chapter."

Rocco Morelli

CEO, Recombinetics

"*Career with Purpose* is a powerful 'career compass' for navigating the stages of your career. It's jammed with tangible advice you can immediately use to find a job—or even a new career—that gives you purpose."

Mel Adkinson

Director, HR Shared Services

Briggs & Stratton Corporation

"This book really hits the mark as an accurate, well researched, and especially relevant master class for careers today. Grubich and Milsted offer thorough yet concise guidance for every stage of a career or job transition. The provocative usage of the word 'career' as a verb, as in the clever title of the book, demands the reader reframe their short- and long-term relationship with 'work' and 'jobs.' For job searchers of every age, *Career with Purpose* will be an invaluable aid navigating career strategies and the employment marketplace for years to come."

Mina Brown, MCC, CNTC, BCC, MBA

Founder and President, Positive Coaching Solutions, LLC

"Challenging your thinking is exactly what you will receive by choosing to invest time into *Career with Purpose*. The storytelling will reach into your deepest thoughts and reflections creating clarity and practical planning to rediscover your purpose."

Janet Agnello
Vice President of Human Resources
Ellsworth Corporation

"If you are considering a career change, this book is a must read. It provides all the valuable insights and questions that a professional career coach would offer but at your own pace. Identify what it is that you would truly love to do for a living and use their guidance and exercises to discern what is right and unique to you."

Julie Davis
Vice President, People Strategy
Association of Equipment Manufacturers

"Grubich and Milsted's message is clear-cut and succinct. Wherever you are on your career journey, the opportunity is in front of you to find your purpose, discover what you really love doing, and pursue your purpose until you achieve it. It will take courage and confidence but the result of self-satisfaction will be well worth the journey. A great read and a must read for everyone wherever they are on their career path!"

Don Klenk
Vice President, Operations
Zero Zone, Inc.

"Embark on a trip of self-discovery with Grubich and Milsted to 'careering with purpose.' Get out of the rut of doing what you feel like you should do or others think is best for you. We all deserve making time to find our greater meaning and best of all, happiness, in our career choice. This book includes easy to use tools and the inspiration to look inward and ask yourself tough questions to assess your career decisions and what direction will lead you to your best self."

Jenny Hart
Vice President, Human Resources
Carmex Laboratories, Inc.

"Career with Purpose" is the complete guide to uncovering what matters most to you and making a career of it. Grubich and Milsted's career guide is filled with methods and practices from brand-building, to interviewing and negotiating from a position of strength, to onboarding with success. A must read for anyone considering the next steps in their career."

Rachele Lehr
Chief Human Resources Officer
Mayville Engineering Company, Inc.

Dedication

This book is dedicated to those who seek fulfillment in the work they do; to anyone who has sought out the purpose of work in their life; to those who desire having a meaningful impact through their work; and to anyone looking to create a legacy beyond what they do.
This book is dedicated to those …

-   who are driven by purpose and have a hunger to align their career with their purpose—what is most important to them.

-   who are active learners with a desire to learn, grow, and find purpose in the work they do.

-   who are willing to give their strength to others so that they may have the strength to stand on their own.

-   who are humble enough to understand their gaps and have the courage to make a change.

-   who intentionally choose their happiness and enjoyment in the work they do above anything else.

Table of Contents

Acknowledgments

This book is inspired by the thousands of professionals we have collectively worked with through the years. Our highest level of satisfaction comes from seeing individuals identify their strengths and link their purpose to the work that they do.

A special thanks to those who have supported us through the journey of our careers. To those who have helped us find our purpose and to clarify not only what we do but why we do it. So many have influenced each step of our own working lives that we will be forever grateful for the impact they have had on us and their contributions to our success.

We are especially grateful to our colleagues at LAK Group. We talk about doing things with purpose throughout this book, and we are very lucky to work with wonderfully talented professionals who are committed to purpose and providing the best experience possible for our clients and customers.

Finally, we want to acknowledge the support of our families and close friends for the love and encouragement given to us throughout our careers. Knowing you were always there for us and pushing us to consider what it takes to be fulfilled, not just satisfied, at work makes this journey worthwhile.

Introduction

Do you enjoy your work? Do you rise out of bed each morning with drive and energy, already formulating your plans for the day?

Many of the people who come to us seeking guidance and advice on finding a new job or changing careers to renew that lost drive often speak of an emptiness in their work. They confide in us that what they do for a living is unsatisfying and has no real meaning for them. They openly admit that their work doesn't serve a greater purpose for them or for others. Nor does it reflect who they are and what they're capable of doing.

What we find is not surprising. People will often jump at a job or a career opportunity for the short-term gain. They'll enter a job interview singularly focused on the tangibles: title, salary, and benefits. They'll be made an offer and soon discover that the role doesn't measure up to their expectations or there are mismatches with management and culture. They don't see a path forward in that new organization and in less than two years, they'll change jobs again and lament how they can't find satisfaction and fulfillment in their work.

What is the purpose of work in your life? You spend one-third of your existence laboring at something; a third of it sleeping; and a third spending time with family or engaged in personal activities that have value to you. Understanding the meaning that you want to derive and the impact that you want to make in that working third is incredibly important. What makes it even more significant is that it allows you to give of yourself and derive greater value from the other two-thirds of your life.

Does what you're working at for a living add value to your life?

If you begin your job or career search with that as your quest, then you're on a path to a purpose-driven career. Think longer-term. You don't want to day-trade your working life by buying into and out of titles and compensation packages and using those gains as your metrics for how you grow and develop as an individual. Many people today are focused so intently on short-term advances that they've totally neglected their deepest dreams and ambitions. It's hard to get out of bed on a Monday morning when you lack the determination and conviction that come from working toward something that has meaning and consequence to you.

Our aim in bringing this book together is to help you, as we have helped many others, define what's important to you in your work life, find your True North, and follow your path with intention and conviction. This is what it means to *career with purpose*.

In our work, we don't view a career as a noun or a thing that you enter into each day and let happen to you over the course of your working life, bouncing from one position to another or climbing a ladder up a wall prescribed to you by someone else. We approach career as a verb, an ongoing pursuit of your own choosing and working at the things that *you* want to accomplish. Seeing as how you're going to spend one-third of your life working, doing it with an intent and clarity of direction will bring greater meaning to your work and greater value to the balance of your life.

If you're in the job market or looking to change careers, before you begin making deliberate choices, look inside yourself and come to terms with what it is that you truly enjoy doing. What is it that maximizes who you are and what you are capable of being? That dream could be and should be your reality.

As our title indicates, this is your guide to finding the work you love. The stories, tools, and exercises within are designed to unearth your authentic story, help you define what it is that you want to do for a living, and make it your brand. We provide the methods to build a sustainable network of inner circle support around you. We give you the strategies that will put you in charge of the interview process and lay out how you can prepare for and act during negotiations. We then help you onboard with purpose, develop a personal development plan, secure early wins, and become an integral part of your new organization.

To career with purpose is to empower yourself. We encourage you to be present and deliberate about the choices you make and the direction you take. So many people just allow their careers to happen to them, and they go with the flow. We challenge you to be more deliberate, starting now.

What you will find in the chapters to follow are the thought models and tools you'll need to prepare you for your journey, to help you better define your purpose, and to provide you the steps to take to achieve your goal. Our book will take you through the same inquiry process and exercises we engage in with our clients. At the end of each chapter, we provide questions to reflect on as you move forward with us and focus in on your ultimate goal. Reflect deeply on each of the questions and be genuine in your responses.

Make your next move the best move of your career. Know your true story, build your personal brand around it, find an organization and culture you can align with, and work at what you love. This time, it will be different.

Michael Grubich and Mike Milsted

1

What Is the Purpose of Your Career?

"The two most important days in your life
are the day you are born and the day you find out why."
—Mark Twain

It was orientation day and Dr. Helen Blackwell, an invited guest speaker for the past several years, got up early to review her speech to the incoming class of medical students. She reflected on how her parents, both of whom were doctors, encouraged and prepared Helen from a very early age to enter the field of medicine. She recalled how one of her first birthday gifts when she was just a toddler was a toy stethoscope, and when she entered kindergarten, a chemistry set for Christmas.

As she sat there waiting her turn to speak, she realized that the medical life was never really her choice from the start. Her parents may have had the best of intentions, but they were teaching her what to think and what career choices to make right out of the gate instead of encouraging her to learn and discover herself and her own realm of possibilities.

Treating people and saving lives was meaningful to Helen, but after 20 years in the profession, she felt adrift. There was an emptiness inside. Although her career and all the work she was doing had such deep meaning for her, she felt there had to be something more to her life. A path toward something. As she addressed the audience, all she wanted to tell these young people was to not become doctors unless it was connected with a greater career purpose.

Pew Research Center conducted two separate surveys in late 2017 to measure what makes Americans' lives feel meaningful, fulfilling, or satisfying. The most popular answer by 69 percent of respondents was family—family makes life most meaningful. After family, 34 percent said their career brought the most meaning to their lives, followed by money, spirituality and faith, and friends.[1]

It stands to reason a career would be at the top of the list: one-third of human life is spent working, and we work at our careers for 35+ years, hoping to derive some sense of fulfillment for all that time invested. Yet, in our practice, we come across many people from all walks of life with careers that they say have meaning, but lack purpose and direction, as is the case of Dr. Blackwell.

To Career with Purpose

Our goal in writing this book is to help you, as we have helped countless others such as Helen and the individuals you'll meet in the chapters to follow, define what's important to you in your work life, find your career path, and follow it with intention. This is what we mean by careering with purpose. In our work, we don't view a career as a noun or a thing that you enter into each day and let happen to you. We treat a career as a verb, an ongoing pursuit of your own volition, and doing the things that *you* want to accomplish. Seeing as how you're going to spend one-third of your life working, doing it with an intent and clarity of direction will bring greater meaning to your work and greater satisfaction and happiness into your life.

It's never too late. There's no time limit on your quest. You could be just starting out, or be in the middle or near the end of your career. You could be entering retirement but want to do so with an intent to take your talents and experience and extend your purpose to serve a cause or to serve your community. However, before you can make deliberate choices about the direction of your career, you have to look inside yourself and come to terms with what it is that you truly enjoy doing and that brings you the greatest satisfaction. What is it that maximizes who you are and what you're capable and desirous of being? What honestly inspires you and drives you?

Wherever you are in your career, the sooner you discover and come to terms with what you really love doing, the sooner you can take the rudder, bring purpose to your career, and become an active participant in determining your own heading and navigating your own work life.

An important part of your discovery process is understanding how you've come to be in the career that you're currently in and knowing what influenced your decision. To help you in your own self-exploration, let's look at examples of people whose career choices at different stages of their lives were misguided and how and why it happened. We'll also share examples of people whose career choices were made for the right reasons and the self-discovery they went through that led them to their ultimate decisions.

For All the Wrong Reasons

Andrew's family owned one of the largest florist shops in the Tampa Bay area, and throughout his high school and college years, his job was that of the bookkeeper for the family business. It wasn't that Andrew loved book-keeping, he simply did it out of necessity. The family needed someone to manage the books and the responsibility fell on his shoulders. He became very proficient at it as a result.

It led Andrew to major in accounting in college, and after years of climbing his accounting ladder, he earned the position of CFO for a major appliance chain. He carved out a comfortable career in finance, but it was never what he really wanted to do. There were other occupations that would have held more meaning and could have given Andrew a greater sense of fulfillment, but his work life story was written for him early on by well-meaning parents who needed help.

Patrick was a third-generation firefighter. His father, grandfather, and great-grandfather were all firemen serving the city of Chicago. The family legacy of fighting fires and saving lives was the only reason Patrick became a firefighter. There were other career paths Patrick thought about when he was younger, all aimed at serving the community, but he shelved them out of a sense of obligation and to fulfill his father's and grandfather's expectations.

The first guidance we gave Andrew and Patrick was to reflect back on the possible vocations they shelved years ago to gain a deeper understanding of why those potential career choices would have been more fulfilling for them.

That inquiry process then involved unearthing what it was about being responsible for a major chain's finances or being a firefighter that they enjoyed the most. What aspect or aspects of their careers, we asked, did they find intellectually or emotionally fulfilling, even if small in significance? We often advise people who come to us with careers that feel empty and directionless to first consider ways of bringing greater purpose to their existing work by reflecting on "why" they do what they do and not just on "what" they do. This is an important first step prior to updating resumes immediately and reviewing open job postings.

Finding that intersection of career choice and purpose is not an easy task. However, the thought exercise is important in that it forces you to look inward to understand how you got to where you are and what your next step forward should be. It requires questions such as the ones you'll find at the end of this chapter and throughout our book to help you uncover the motivations within you that are either facilitating or inhibiting your efforts to find a career with purpose.

The Need for Purpose

We believe that having purpose in one's career is one of the defining characteristics of human beings and an essential component of a fulfilling life. When you have a sense of purpose, you tend not to approach each day with uncertainty and indifference. When you have purpose, life becomes less complicated and less stressful. You become more focused and your mind becomes watertight to your own true story with less space for negative thoughts to leak in.

A powerful example of this can be found in Victor Frankl's famous book, *Man's Search for Meaning*, in which Frankl, a Holocaust survivor, describes his experiences in concentration camps during the Second World War. Frankl, who was an Austrian neurologist and psychiatrist at the time of his capture, observed that the inmates who were most likely to survive were those who felt they had a goal or purpose.[2]

There has been much research on the value of purpose in people's lives. One of the most famous studies, published in the *Journal of the*

American Medical Association, analyzed data from the 27-year-old Health and Retirement Study (a U.S.-based, nationally representative well-being longitudinal study involving close to 7,000 people) and found that living and working with meaning and a sense of purpose was the greatest contributor to living longer lives. A sense of purpose was also linked to happiness, fulfillment, and maximum productivity at work.[3]

It makes one wonder, why do people jump at career opportunities for the wrong reasons? More often than not, people will quit their companies for more compensation or a greater title. It's similar to day-trading. You might realize short-term gains, but in the long run, you could regret the quick decisions you made along the way.

Satisfiers and Dissatisfiers

We often pose this question to the people we work with, whether they're CEOs or new hires: *"Imagine it's Sunday night. What mood are you in as you think about going into work on Monday?"* How you answer this could either be motivated by feelings of get up and go, indifference and disinterest, or no feelings at all. It's hard to get out of bed and want to take on the day with enthusiasm and energy when you have little or no interest in what you're doing.

The reason for this may be explained in the research found in Frederick Herzberg's *Motivation to Work*, which focuses on our satisfiers and dissatisfiers.[4] Herzberg reasons that because the factors causing satisfaction are different from those causing dissatisfaction, the two feelings simply cannot be treated as opposites of one another. The opposite of satisfaction is not dissatisfaction but rather no satisfaction. Similarly, the opposite of dissatisfaction is not satisfaction but rather no dissatisfaction.

So, what does this mean when it comes to career choices? You need to look for those things that drive satisfaction in your career. Don't simply make decisions based on elements that dissatisfy you. Identify those things that are important to you and instill motivation and purpose in you. These are your satisfiers that you should have in mind in your search for the right job or career.

We believe having a career with purpose helps build significance in our daily lives. We become less self-centered and feel a part of something bigger, something outside of ourselves. This makes us less focused on our own worries and anxieties. Purpose gives us a constant source of activity to channel our mental energies and spend less time in distracted thought. We become more productive and collaborative in the service of something of greater value to ourselves and to others. Does your work liberate that feeling and energy in you?

For All the Right Reasons

What if your purpose was to become your work? Every day and step of the way would become meaningful. Your career journey would not be just an aimless wandering or something determined by someone else and assigned to you. Instead, what you do for a living would become an outcropping of your nature, chosen by you and therefore very genuine and instinctively you.

We work with many executives who, after having climbed the rungs of their career ladders for years or even decades, have come to realize that they want to use their talents, skills, and connections to have a greater positive impact on themselves and their families, and often for their communities. Chris, as example, became a financial advisor out of college and ultimately a financial planning executive for his company. After twenty years of promotions and advancements, he began to question if he wanted to climb that same ladder for another ten or more years.

Chris had always been involved with the community he lived in and came to realize in the middle of his career that serving the public was his greater purpose. He started firefighting training on weekends and evenings, fulfilling a long-time calling that he had never before answered. He ultimately walked away from his career in finance and is now successfully leading an emergency dispatch center in the Chicagoland area. By looking inward, Chris eventually found a career that meant something to him.

Finding the courage to question your career decisions is not an easy task, but it's one you must take in order to find your inner purpose. It will feel risky and change can sometimes be frightening, but every time, and we mean absolutely <u>every time</u>, people who have gone through their inquiry process have found true satisfaction with their career choice.

Mary is another example of someone scratching a vocational itch and satisfying a desire or need for something greater out of her working life. Her mom and dad were both schoolteachers, and the one piece of advice that they gave her that weighed heavy in her mind as she began getting serious about college and a career was to *not* become a teacher. Deep down inside though, Mary loved the notion of teaching for a living. She always wanted to lead and instruct others, but she heeded her parents' advice and entered the field of marketing instead. She fell into the trap of letting others, although well-meaning, determine her future and becoming what they thought she should or shouldn't become.

Mary's growing feelings of dissatisfaction prompted her to go through her own inquiry process, leading her to apply for a career development position in her company's HR department. She realizes it's not the same as teaching a class of middle-school students, which will remain her dream, but it does scratch that "teaching" itch for her, allowing her to be an instructor of sorts and a guidance counselor as well and build a new career that had more meaning for her and greater personal satisfaction.

There are many ways to scratch your vocational itch without completely changing careers. You can use your talents and skills to make your current work life more determined and fulfilling. It all begins with understanding what is most important to you that will have you springing out of bed each morning excited to go into work and make a difference in your life or in the lives of others.

Monica is an executive chef for three of her city's most expensive restaurants. She loves her work, but for the past few years, her growing concern for the homeless in her community has discomforted her and detached her from her passion for cooking. She was preparing meals the cost of which would fill shopping carts with food, not to mention the huge amount of food waste that was simply disposed of at the end of every shift in each of her restaurants.

Monica put a simple business plan together and received both government and private funding to create a non-profit startup to collect wasted food from restaurants and distribute it to food banks. She began with one van and one driver and now her non-profit has a fleet of vans and a management team. Monica's career now couldn't be more fulfilling to her.

There are many people like Monica who often come to us mentally blocked in their ability to recognize what it is that truly matters to them and brings them enjoyment. They discover how their talents and skills can be of value to something greater than themselves, yielding in return a greater sense of satisfaction in their day-to-day work.

Mark is a general contractor for a company that builds private dwellings in his city. Although he loves working with his hands and being responsible for overseeing the day-to-day activities of construction projects, he wanted to construct something even greater. Through his own inquiry process, Mark found a way to contribute to his community by using his talents and skills on weekends to build homes for Habitat for Humanity. Giving something back to his city has made all the difference in Mark's outlook on his career and has created new opportunities for even greater community service.

Managing Expectations

Many parents with young children will know of the tales of Hermey the Elf, a character originating in the 1964 film *Rudolph the Red-Nosed Reindeer*. Hermey wants to be a dentist but doesn't want to be an elf. He just wasn't getting any joy out of being an elf. The moral of this story for children and adults is to follow your heart. Yet, things can get in the way and our expectations of ourselves or others' expectations of us take us off our path or set us off in the wrong direction.

At some point, you have to address the stories that you've chosen to believe about who you are and what your value is. You have to come to terms with what you've heard over your lifetime and chosen to believe about what you can and can't do. It's time that stopped. It's you who gets to choose the stories that you believe or not believe and choose to act upon or not. It's time for you to write your own story, define your own purpose, and use that outcome as your bearing for your career. An important part of that process is managing expectations.

Managing Your Expectations of Yourself

The art of managing expectations begins by having an honest discussion with yourself and giving deep consideration to what you want to achieve in that one-third of your life. Begin by asking yourself what you like and dislike most about your job and career direction.

When we create expectations of ourselves in our minds that don't turn out exactly as we hoped, we often feel disappointment and even shame, believing we should have been better, smarter, or more prepared. Your failed expectations, however, do not have to be obstacles to your happiness.

Take stock of the things that you've accomplished in your life. What roles and activities over the years have you performed exceedingly well? What comes natural to you and brings you the greatest enjoyment and sense of personal satisfaction? Those are clearly your strengths. Coming from a place of realism, positivity, and confidence in this way allows you to move forward with your expectations of yourself as a companion instead of an advisor. The question is: are you leveraging those strengths now?

Managing the Expectations of Others

We all struggle at different degrees with living up to the expectations of others, whether they're our friends, colleagues at work, or loved ones. Expectations of others begin when we're born with our parents setting rules for how we should behave and contribute around the house.

It never really ends. From kindergarten on, there are educational and performance standards that we have to meet in order to advance to middle school, then high school, then on to college. And when we begin our careers in the real world, our bosses and peers expect us to be productive.

Expectations aren't bad in and of themselves. They're placed on us throughout our lives to challenge and encourage us. They're a natural part of the human condition. We all need and want encouragement. The problem arises when we place too much emphasis on the expectations of others to the point where we're living and performing to meet their standards and their approval.

Others' expectations of what your career should be are seldom a true measure of what is right for you. In truth, their expectations aren't based on who you are and your life experiences, but on their own experiences. They're looking at your life through their lens, not yours. Others' expectations of you, regardless of how close they are to you, don't take into account your true talents, inclinations, and desires, or what is even possible or realistic for you.

The key is centering yourself around what's most important to you. When it comes to your career, you need to own it and be a bit selfish about it because it is all about you and what you want and expect of yourself, not what others expect of you. This is a key stop in your journey and it's important that you look internally to what will drive your overall career satisfaction.

Managing Societal Expectations

The expectations brought on by the world we live in are the most difficult to contend with or rise above. For a young person, social pressure comes from all corners such as family, school, friends, friends' parents, movies, and music. Probably the most significant area of influence on young people and societal expectations today is social media.

As example, for generations, young people have been directed to believe that they must go to college in order to succeed in life. To that end, high schools, colleges, and universities became singularly focused on counseling students to do well on their SATs (Scholastic Achievement Test) and ACTs (American College Testing), find a college or university, and get accepted. SAT and ACT testing requirements paused during the COVID-19 pandemic and are now permanently optional at some universities. However, the vast majority at this time still require aptitude testing.

The day after he turned eighteen, Anthony began applying to universities just as every one of his friends did. Uncertain where he wanted to go to college or what he wanted to major in, he covered his bases by filling out and submitting a stack of college applications. He would then decide on a major later.

Anthony had a passion for mechanical things since the age of three when he built his first go-cart. He didn't need an SAT score to go to a technical college; mechanics was his natural aptitude. What brought him the greatest joy was having a wrench in his hand. But many young people fearing social pressure are afraid to say they're considering technical school instead of a four-year institution.

If it weren't for the expectations of society, college would not have been Anthony's choice of next steps after high school, nor for millions of other young people, we would imagine. College is not always the right answer for everyone. Anthony ultimately got his associate's degree in aircraft maintenance and now is a certified aircraft mechanic making a great living with the freedom on weekends to build and race go-carts with his son.

We often use the phrase "be intentional" when it comes to your career. Seek to understand what's important to you. Be deliberative and truly take the time to define it and align yourself with it.

Getting Deliberate About Your Career

The role of work in the lives of so many people today looks and behaves so different than it did just two years ago. The 2020 pandemic enacted significant change in the way companies do business and accelerated the development of technologies to enable virtual work. It also shifted commerce even more dramatically toward online shopping and services.

People are viewing their work lives through a new lens now and are able to participate uniquely in their careers as never before. People who shelved their talents and personal interests years ago (or even decades ago) because they couldn't build livelihoods around their dreams can do so now with technology as their enabler. You can hike Olympic National Park, pitch a tent for an office, and find enough Wi-Fi to work on your project.

Throughout our book, we will help you understand the various elements that can help you on your career journey and provide you with the thought models and tools you need to career with purpose.

The intent of our book is to encourage you to step back and take the time to identify what it is that you would truly love to do for a living and help you synthesize what is right and unique to you. So, before you start updating your resume and LinkedIn page, evaluating companies, and begin interviewing for your next career, let's do it with purpose. Let's determine together what your true north is and what's important to you so there are no missteps along the way and your next career decision is the decision for a lifetime.

What you will find in the chapters to follow are the thought models and tools you'll need to prepare you for your journey, to help you better define your purpose, and to provide you the steps to take to achieve your goal. Our book will take you through the same inquiry process we engage in with our clients. In each chapter, we'll provide questions to reflect on as you move forward with us and focus in on your ultimate goal. Reflect deeply on each of the questions and be genuine in your responses. Have this become your workbook and diary of your journey to a career with purpose.

Questions to Reflect On

1. Whose expectations have influenced your careers over the years?

2. What would you love to do most for a living? Does it in any way connect to what you're doing now? How could those paths join for you?

3. What do you feel is missing in your current role or the career you're pursuing?

4. What were the essential elements of a past job experience or role that felt successful for you and, in turn, made you feel satisfied and proud of your work effort?

5. What are three essential elements of your current job or role that you feel hinder or impede your success and make you feel unsatisfied at times, or all the time?

6. If you knew you couldn't fail, what is something you want to achieve in the next 12 months?

2

"Sign, Sign, Everywhere a Sign"

"If you don't know where you're going, any road will take you there."
—Lewis Carroll

People are viewing their work lives differently nowadays and are able to participate directly and purposefully in their careers as never before. Wherever you are on your career journey, the sooner you discover and come to terms with what you really love doing, the sooner you can take the wheel, bring meaning to your career, and become an active participant in navigating your own work life.

Knowing your purpose helps you distinguish what to look for and how to read the signs along the way. The better you are at defining where you want to be and what you want to be doing, the better you'll be at interpreting the messages that will appear on your journey. As you're reading these messages, try not to regard them as a this-job-or-that-job or this-company-or-that-company proposition. It's what you want your work life experience to be, namely, doing the work that enables you to grow and develop in the areas that have the greatest meaning to you, and doing so in an organizational culture that aligns with your values and interests.

Everywhere a Sign

The title of this chapter borrows a fitting lyric from the 1970s song "Signs" by the Five Man Electrical Band. Seeking out signs is an essential characteristic of humans. We do it to confirm our beliefs, authenticate our journeys, and keep us from harm. In the context of careering with purpose, however, some signs aren't as straightforward in meaning or even visible to us at first. They're easy to miss if we're narrowly focused on something else; or we see the sign but find it difficult to imagine or accept its message at that moment in our lives.

It was early in Mark's career when he was presented with an opportunity to enter into a business partnership with James, a business mentor and long-time friend. It was at a point in James's life where he was looking to sell his business and retire and asked Mark, a colleague he could trust, if he wanted to buy into it. Mark politely declined, *"Thank you, but no thank you, James. That really isn't an area of interest or the direction I want to take right now."*

Although the nature of the business aligned with Mark's career heading long term, he wasn't able to decipher that maybe James's offer was something he should consider at this point in time. James was patient and suggested that he and Mark have lunch once a month just to keep the conversation open. Mark agreed, and to his surprise, within six months he found himself in serious negotiations with James about becoming his business partner.

Mark ultimately brought in an additional partner to buy out the business entirely from James, who could retire now knowing his small enterprise was in good hands. While Mark wasn't able to read the sign correctly at first, he remained open to the proposition because it aligned with where he ultimately wanted to be in his career. That exploration over the next six months was all about Mark looking inward and determining exactly what he wanted out of his work life; and looking outward, with the help of James, to assess the growth potential of the industry and makeup of the marketplace.

You can never know for certain what's around the corner while on your journey. You have to stay focused and true to your dream, yet be attentive and wise to the signs that will appear along the way. Some will be tempting. The key is not allowing yourself to be persuaded by title, salary, perks, or benefits, but at the same time, being open to opportunities that may parallel your path, or even accelerate it. What helps with staying focused yet remaining open is understanding the impact that you want to make and measuring everything against that outcome. Mark wasn't crystal clear on what impact he wanted his career to have and it was during those six months that he was able to define his purpose and goals more succinctly.

James accelerated Mark's inward/outward/forward career examination (a model that we'll share later in this chapter), by asking him thoughtful questions about what effect he wanted to have through his work and what he enjoyed doing the most. There were other people in Mark's life who were closer to him than James, but they each had established beliefs about what they thought Mark wanted, or should want, out of his work life. James was more of a neutral, fair witness who could challenge Mark's expectations of himself and others' expectations of him.

The more centered you are on what impact you want to make and what brings you the most joy doing, the easier it's going to be for you to judge your career opportunities as being right, not right yet, or wrong altogether. Having a neutral, experienced friend or colleague can clear away the blind spots and sharpen your vision. We'll speak more on your network of business associates as a valuable asset later in this chapter and devote the entirety of Chapter 8 on the ways in which networking can become the secret sauce in your career or job search.

What Causes Our Blind Spots

We all have blind spots, often created by the expectations we spoke of in Chapter 1: the expectations we place upon ourselves, the expectations that family and friends place upon us, and the expectations of society. Any of these has the potential to cause your career to happen to you instead of you directing your career.

For some, their greatest blind spot is fear of the unknown. Many others simply lack the courage or conviction to trust their abilities to undertake and accomplish something different or truly challenging. Many distrust themselves as the result of the stories they chose to believe about who they are and what they're capable of. What also prevents people from taking action is their unwillingness to acknowledge and accept what the signs might be telling them, even if those signs are right.

We had a client we were working with who had a career-changing experience that demonstrates this blind spot concept. The new product development department in her company was disbanded after the departure of the vice president of marketing. Sarah, one of the star employees of the small group, was offered an associate brand manager position in the brand development department. She flatly turned it down because she read it as a half-step backward. Sarah was more concerned about others' perception of her not progressing fast enough and ended up saying no to an opportunity to grow in a different direction though still in her fields of interest: research, brand development, and marketing. She had a complete blind spot because she was more concerned about the short-term impact on how others perceive her, versus the long-term impact of increasing her scope and breadth of skills for future roles. She took a fixed mindset into a situation versus a career growth mindset.

Blind spots inhibit our ability to make balanced decisions that will have a long-term impact on our career. Factors including salary, incentives, perks, title, status, and even job location limit the ability of many to make a balanced decision about their career. It is critical that every individual takes some time to evaluate and reflect on their purpose, career objective, and overall plan.

What's your career trip plan? You don't drive from Seattle to Tampa Bay without having calculated a route. There are going to be stops along the way, detours, and even points of interest where you'll want to spend extra time. What is your roadmap and what signs are you looking out for to confirm that you're on the right path?

The Grass May Look Greener

Many people enter their careers nowadays practicing a policy of staying at a job for two to three years, then moving on to greener pastures. Not everyone wants to be a 10-year, 12-year, or 15-year employee in the same company. People oftentimes get frustrated in their job or with their company, or with the pace of things, and make conscious decisions to change their situations.

In our experience, many who find themselves in these positions are acting out an emotion or belief, or running from something or someone like a bad boss, versus running toward something more meaningful and personally fulfilling. Most often, they find that the jobs and organizations that they ran to have as many flaws as the ones they were escaping from.

Once that frustration sets in, for reasons that may be real or imagined, people will begin rationalizing and building to their decision point through a mental process that, in a way, resembles the accumulation of strikes in the game of baseball:

Strike 1: they get frustrated and then they get over it.
Strike 2: they get frustrated again but are still standing at the plate saying, *"If it happens again, I'm outta here."*
Strike 3: they finally decide, *"That's it! If I find something, anything, I'll leave."*

Susan was a highly paid, successful in-house attorney in the banking industry. She grew frustrated though after a couple of years over the legal remit process of waiting for judgments and decisions on her filings. She was at strike three in her mind and decided to stay in the industry but change companies and pursue a career in business development.

After six months, she discovered that her new role primarily involved selling banking services to business-to-business prospects and managing client relationships. She found herself adding no value to the process nor learning any new, marketable skills. What really upset her was that she was no longer challenged intellectually as she was as a corporate attorney. It was the mental challenge that she loved the most but didn't realize it until it was gone.

Susan is now considering moving into a different area within the same industry. It requires her starting at the bottom with a sizeable pay cut and on an uncertain career path. Alternatively, she could leave the industry and try to restart her legal profession elsewhere. Susan's career change decision brought her a great deal of unhappiness and uncertainty. She now realizes that her motivations for changing careers may have been shortsighted.

We've all experienced days on the job being easier than others or had setbacks to our work or progress. You may find yourself wondering whether your job and your place of work are still right for you and your goals, or if it's time for a change. So how do you distinguish between when you just need greater patience on your part, or if you're at strike three and it's time to start seriously looking for other opportunities?

Cautionary Signs to Look Out For

Finding a fulfilling career can be a long, stepwise journey. Few people enter the workforce knowing exactly what they want to do. In fact, by age 50, the average person will have held 12 different jobs in their efforts to find the "right fit." For many, this requires changing careers completely.[5]

You have to be certain and read the right signs correctly to know if changing jobs or changing careers is a good move for you. Here are what we believe to be the cautionary signs that you should look out for—the internal and external indicators that it may be time for a job or career change. Though these are the most common signals, how they affect you personally or appear in your work environment will vary depending on your personal situation. How you react to them will vary as well depending on your thresholds and resilience to setbacks and frustrations.

The **internal signs** tend to center on those things that have personal meaning and value to you.

Stress levels have become unbearable – People will often put up with a stressful job for the title or the pay, but it never fails to take its toll. Over time, ailments related to stress, and there are many, may seriously jeopardize your health and quality of life.

Sunday is spent dreading Monday – It's hard to discern between short-term dissatisfaction and a deep-seated unhappiness, but if you go to bed every night and wake up every morning upset with what you do or where you work, it may be time to look for a change.

You're not feeling challenged – People can hit plateaus over the course of their careers. Even exciting jobs can become boring. Work routines can become monotonous and you don't see much opportunity around you to build on your skills and experience.

No clear path for your career – You're aware of the meaning and purpose you want out of your career, but your current job and upward or even lateral moves are not available in your department or anywhere across the company.

Not feeling valued – At some point in our working lives, we feel as if our manager or co-workers just don't appreciate us. Signs of not being valued are when you do great work and don't get credit for it, or co-workers don't give you the support you need.

Work/life imbalance – Career fulfillment and happiness cannot offset poor work/life balance. Working longer hours or feeling pressured to take work home with you because of job responsibilities begins encroaching on your personal time.

Not all signs are internal. There are also **external signs** that can cause you to reevaluate your situation. Circumstances or changes can emanate from management practices, your relationship with your boss or peers, or the status of the company, industry, or marketplace.

You don't get along with your boss – People will often put up with a bad manager as long as the job pays well, but if the money and benefits aren't there, many will leave their job because their managers don't respect them, intimidate them, or fail to trust them.

Leadership can't be trusted – Not liking your boss is bad enough; not trusting them is far worse. A number of factors can contribute to that distrust such as your superiors being ineffective, incompetent, unreliable, or even deceitful.

The work environment is detrimental – The culture of the company or your team or what your company offers the marketplace doesn't align with your values. Staying in this kind of environment can take its toll on your psyche if you're compromising your values.

You've reached a pay ceiling – You may have reached a salary cap for your current position and see no opportunities for promotion. There's only so much negotiating you can do if you've reached an upper limit and your employer can't or won't work with you.

You're passed over for promotions – When this happens, find out why. You may not have the right certification or training or you may lack the experience. Asking shows you want more responsibility. But if you don't get a straight answer, it might be something more.

The company is having rounds of layoffs – It's a vulnerable feeling to have your position in jeopardy. Layoffs can happen to any company. They're not always easy to predict, but if a reduction in force is forthcoming, consider that a salient warning sign.

Whether these signs appear and how you choose to read them will be unique to you and your situation. The question is, at what point does a sign turn into a story that calls for action on your part? Many times, these internal and external indicators will occur in unison and to varying degrees of effect. As example, not getting along with your boss is one thing, but having an adversarial relationship with them is unhealthy and non-productive. If that results in you being overlooked for a promotion and leads you to believe that you can't trust your manager or the company's leadership, then there may be something systemically wrong about you working there.

Framework for Reading the Signs

Merging your understanding of the kind of job and career that you most desire with the signs that appear along the way can be a challenging undertaking for anyone. This is made even more challenging nowadays given the new technologies that can impact where you work, how you work, and what you can now define as "work" or a "career." You have to be your own best navigator along your journey and know the terrain that you're presently in or entering for the first time.

We believe our <u>Framework for Career Discussions</u> provides a proper model for planning your trip and for reading the signs when they appear. Our framework consists of three exercises that require thoughtful consideration: *Looking Inward* to discover your desired work characteristics; *Looking Outward* to incorporate information on the company, industry, and marketplace direction; and *Looking Forward* to set goals and create your own action plan as a result of what you discovered about yourself and your environment.

Let's explore each to understand how applying this disciplined and objective thought process to your career or job search can help you find that sweet spot where you *Career with Purpose* by being genuine about your work life objectives, unbiased and honest in your assessment of your current environment, and open-minded and positive about the path ahead.

Framework for Career Discussions

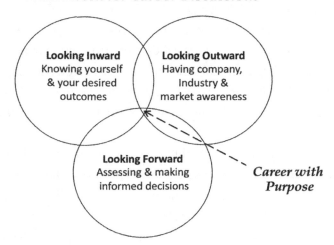

Looking Inward

The internal motivation for reading your own signs has to be there first. What makes you happy or unhappy in your work life? Do you feel a sense of purpose and meaning in what you do for a living? Looking inward is all about knowing yourself and the outcomes of your work that are the most satisfying for you.

What are the work tasks that you enjoy the most and why? Think of three recent accomplishments and the skills you used to complete those tasks successfully. Does your work help you develop those skills or learn new skills in those areas? What talents do you have that you would like to develop that are not utilized in your present situation?

What is your reputation with your peers, colleagues, management, and customers? Do you feel a sense of belonging? Are you respected for your contributions and do you have colleagues that you enjoy working with and make you better at what you do? Do you find value-alignment and personal satisfaction in the products and services that you help bring to the marketplace? Do you feel you deliver value to your customers?

We had a client, Kathy, who was struggling with what she wanted to do next in her career. She had a great job as a principal of a Catholic grade school, loved the people she was working with, and her job was close to home. Even with these elements, she didn't feel satisfaction in her role as an educator. She loved teaching others but was ready to do something different. She started looking right away for corporate training and development roles. Her thought was, *"I like teaching, so maybe I should transition to the corporate world."*

Kathy struggled to find the right fit as she could not articulate to others (and frankly herself) why this was a good transition for her career. We had Kathy spend time reflecting and looking inward to find her purpose. She realized that her faith was the key driver of satisfaction and purpose in her life. Eventually, Kathy transitioned into a role at her parish leading faith formation and counseling. Kathy constantly tells us she has found the *"job of my dreams."*

Looking Outward

The next step requires you to research your company, your industry, and the marketplace to help determine your trip plan. When you're looking outward, you have to understand what's going on in the marketplace and how your company performs compared to others in your industry. Is your company positioned to keep pace with market shifts and changing consumer needs and expectations? At a higher level, what are the trends in your industry, especially in terms of new technologies and the global economy that can impact your choice and direction?

How does the culture of your company affect your ability to grow and develop your skills and experience? Is it a positive work environment that prioritizes the well-being of its employees, offers support at all levels within the organization, and has policies in place that encourage respect, trust, empathy, and support? Is it a collaborative environment with passionate people who care about their work and strive to be the best at what they do?

What can be of most value to you when looking outward is to be connected with a diverse network of business associates who have greater knowledge and experience on the trends in your industry. They may also have insights into the abilities of your company and its leadership to meet those challenges.

What's equally valuable is that such a network will challenge your thinking and possibly accelerate your thought processes as James did for Mark in our earlier story by asking Mark self-examining questions about what impact he wanted to make through his work and what he enjoyed working at the most.

Looking Forward

Once you've looked inward to what's important to you and then outward to assess the strength and culture of your present company along with industry and marketplace trends, looking forward is the opportunity to step back and assess what you've discovered in your research and in networking with experienced people. You're now in a position to make an informed decision on where you want to go on your career journey.

Looking forward is also looking within as you weigh your personal goals and desires against the advantages and disadvantages that are presented to you. Is the company you're with enabling your journey? Is it big enough to allow you the vertical climbing space or lateral moves that will allow you to aspire to whatever job you want?

To career with purpose is the sweet spot or outcome of this framework where the result of all your mindful efforts exist: you're doing what you love doing in an environment that inspires, reinforces, and supports you; you're keeping your finger on the pulse of what's going on around you; and you're navigating your own path in a career with resolve and meaning.

People don't always arrive at that sweet spot. Many will only focus inward and neglect the cautionary signs that it's time for change. Others will see the signs but deny their existence out of fear of the unknown or because they lack confidence in themselves. In order to ensure that you're not making a rash decision by staying out of fear or leaving too soon hoping that the grass will be greener, ensure that these three circles of looking inward, outward, and forward are receiving equal attention and deliberation.

Watch for Breadcrumbs

Companies have a way of creating a dependency with their employees with promises that often keep them from leaving their current job for a different position internally or keep them from leaving the company altogether. These assurances keep people so dedicated to their boss or to their team that they miss seeing (or deny seeing) the signs that are telling them that it's time to stand up for themselves.

There's a recent career term called "breadcrumbing" that refers to being strung along at work by a manager who leads an employee to believe that they'll get that raise, promotion, bonus, internal transfer, higher corporate title, or even be moved from a cubicle to an office with a door. However, there's always a reason why it can't happen just right now. Yet, the manager continues to offer enough breadcrumbs to keep the employee from thinking of leaving.[6]

Breadcrumbing could be due to a number of reasons, many of which are valid and well-intended by your manager who's looking out for your personal growth and development. Your manager may not really be sure about your abilities and is attempting to get you motivated and offering breadcrumbs as an enticement to see if you can accomplish difficult goals. Moreover, they may feel that you're just not management material yet and may not want to lose you because of their training investment in you and that you have potential and are worth developing further.

On the other hand, your manager could be breadcrumbing you because they may be manipulative and don't really care about you personally. Perhaps they need you to do the hard, often mundane work that underutilizes your talents, skills, and experience. The boss could be simply stringing you along until they find someone better or cheaper as your replacement. It could also be that your manager is just not that good of a manager or developer of people. They don't realize what they're doing or the dissatisfaction and unhappiness they're building in you. Additionally, the company itself may have plans that don't include you, such as in a relocation or dissolution of a department or division, but they'll need you invested in the job until they can execute those decisions.

To uncover the real signs, expose the truth, and determine if your present situation is working for or against your growth and the development of your career, consider taking the following direct and purposeful steps:

- Ask your manager why they're not delivering on their promises. Find out if there are legitimate financial or business reasons and try to set a timetable for the promises to be met.

- Inquire if there is something that you are not doing correctly or need some help improving. If this is the case, show initiative and ask for that training.

- If improvement to your work product is not the reason, keep track of your accomplishments, particularly when you've exceeded expectations. Share the results of your work with your boss's boss to test the veracity of your manager.

- Consult with other trusted employees to see if this is happening to them as well.

If you discover through this line of inquiry with your manager that you're being taken advantage of and there's no real honest intention of raises, promotions, or more challenging work, then you need to prepare to make your move. Read the signs carefully so you don't hold out for promises that may never come true. You have to be an active and aware participant in your career.

Signs Your Employee Is Looking for a New Job

Maybe you're the well-intended manager we mentioned who's breadcrumbing an employee for valid reasons but they're impatient and looking to leave. These are the telltale signs that your employee may be considering leaving or already has one foot out the door.

- They're using their personal phone more often.
- Performance has slipped and their attendance has dropped.
- They are acting noncommittal and speaking up less at team meetings.
- They're coming to work looking better dressed than usual and taking longer lunches.
- As you walk by their cube or office, you find their LinkedIn screen is up.
- They are distancing themselves from you and their teammates.

It's possible that the above signs can also be an indication that your employee is simply unhappy, whether it's personal or work-related, and is not looking for another job at all. You may need to check in with them to get the full story and find out if there is anything you can do to help.

Questions to Reflect On

1. How do you personally balance staying focused and true to your career path while remaining open to opportunities that may appear around you?

2. What signs do you look for to confirm that you're on the right career path?

3. Where do you draw the line between needing greater patience with your work situation and needing to look for other opportunities?

4. What internal cautionary sign or combination of signs would it take for you to consider a job or career change?

5. What external sign or signs would motivate you to take action and make a change?

6. Proactively, what steps do you take to ensure that the three circles of looking inward, looking outward, and looking forward are receiving equal attention and deliberation and enabling you to career with purpose?

3

The Workplace Is Evolving

"Change your thoughts and you change your world."
—Norman Vincent Peale

Martina has been a bank teller for 15 years and from the start felt it was a smart decision for her and her family. The branch office she works at is close to home, the hours accommodate her busy schedule leaving her evenings free, and her second income added to her husband's helps to pay expenses and save for their children's college fund.

Recently, Martina discovered that her branch is closing as so many have in her city in the past few years. Anxiety is starting to set in as she sees her job and career evaporating before her eyes. It begins to dawn on her the financial stress this action will place on her family. Being a teller is all she's ever done or knows how to do. As she puts it, *"It's the only career I ever wanted because it was simple and perfect. So, what do I do now?"*

More than one million people work at the 10 largest banks in the U.S., an industry currently spending $150 billion a year, more than any other industry in America, to develop labor-saving technology. Wells Fargo, the largest, believes that machines will replace the teller position and plans to eliminate up to 200,000 other banking jobs over the next decade.[7]

Can you remember the last time you walked into a bank and engaged in a financial transaction with a bank teller? Automation and artificial intelligence are quickly replacing this long-standing career for many people. Checks can be deposited directly over your mobile phone and ATMs are increasingly performing more complicated transactions once the domain of human beings only.

While Chapter 1 centered on helping you formulate your thoughts around what's important to you as you pursue a career with purpose, Chapter 3 delves deeper into the *looking outward* and *looking forward* components of the <u>Framework for Career Discussions</u> that we introduced in Chapter 2. We'll speak first to the changing workplace environment—from a new generation in leadership, to a greater focus on employee development and well-being, to flexible working arrangements. We'll then share with you the directions we see the world of work headed over the next several years to better inform your career search.

Let's begin by looking at how the profile of the American workforce itself has fundamentally altered in just the past ten years, the most significant of which is the changing of the guard at the executive and mid-levels of leadership, bringing a new perspective to how work is conducted.

Generations Apart, Yet Together

Much has been written about the differences among the four generations working together today, primarily contrasting their demographics, styles of work, and personal values. Our perspective is that these generational differences are already altering the workplace from what it's been known to be in a number of ways including cultural beliefs about work, a greater focus on people, flexible workplace arrangements, employee development programs, and well-being initiatives. We believe that these dynamics will be the most important to consider when evaluating a company and the opportunities that may exist there for you. Let's briefly look into each of the generations at work today. Though they may vary in age, experience, and values, they are closer than ever in working together and benefiting from each other's perspectives.

Baby boomers are starting careers at a most unexpected time in their lives—at the end of their careers. They may be retiring today at their highest rate as a generation, and the pandemic has certainly accelerated the phasing out of this group, but many are not accepting their 60s as their retirement decade.

We'll cover this in greater detail later in this chapter, but what we see happening is a growing resistance to programmed retirement. Many boomers are wanting to and are capable of staying employed longer than their parents. They're becoming reemployed in a second career, or finding other meaningful, vocational work. There are a number of factors contributing to this non-retirement movement: seniors leading healthier lives, advances in medicine, changing social attitudes about the role of seniors in society, and new technologies that not only enable remote work but allow what were once hobbies to become careers.

We're witnessing companies actually hiring back boomers, not only for the productivity that they bring, which can be equal to or greater than that of younger employees, but more so for their goal orientation, work ethic, and sense of loyalty and commitment. Additionally, companies are hiring seniors for the leadership qualities that they're able to transfer to the younger generations.

Gen Xers bring a unique perspective to work ethic, quality of work life, and reciprocal relationships into the workplace, where hierarchies are flattened and leaders and employees can mutually influence one another. They are the architects of the "productive office space," working environments that foster feelings of creativity and comfort where employees can feel confident and self-expressive. Research has shown that spaces which maximize natural light through large windows make people feel happier and result in less absenteeism, reduced stress, fewer illnesses, and increased employee productivity and alertness.[8]

This change in work environment, structure, and culture is, in part, because this generation currently has the largest influence in the C-Suite, having moved into leadership roles over the last few years to the point now where the majority of people you see on executive teams and in senior positions are Gen Xers and older millennials.

We bring this up because we believe that the leadership of an organization has never been as important as it is today when assessing what place of employment is best for you. Companies that place a strong emphasis on workplace environment typically put an equal importance on employee development and career advancement. That should be a strong consideration for you as you assess the different working environments, values, and talent development opportunities of the companies that are of interest to you.

Millennials are the first generation to pursue a working life that conforms to their personal life and not the other way around. They're making it known that their preferences and expectations will come first and not having their companies define it for them. What's important to note is that their sentiments on work and work-life balance are not just longings. Millennials now pretty much populate the entirety of mid-level leadership and management and have significant influence in making the expectations of work-life balance a reality.

The majority of this group are starting to have families, influencing many to want to remain working remotely or in a hybrid fashion following the restrictions of the 2020 pandemic. Being able to work from home fits the lifestyle of this generation perfectly. How we Gen Xers, the authors of this book, would have loved the place-and-time flexibility that millennials have today: to be able to work from home; to not have to lose an hour of your life commuting each way every day to work; or to be able to take your son to baseball practice or help coach your daughter's high school tennis team.

Thanks to millennials, long gone are the days where you log in eight hours chained to a desk and accomplish the bare minimum until you can clock out at 5:00 p.m. The quality-of-life benefits this generation values outweigh company loyalty. Work-life balance means as much to millennials as health insurance, paid vacations, and retirement plans mean to boomers and Gen Xers. Where millennials differ even more though is the degree to which they value the benefits of work flexibility. Many will consider changing companies in search of specific perks or benefits. But buyer beware. Perks and benefits can mask an organization's true work culture, along with scope of the job and the opportunity to develop and grow.

Megan, a young millennial, is considering leaving her position at her current company for a greater opportunity at another. The new role would be perfect for her given the responsibilities of the new position and its high visibility, not to mention the great pay she would receive and the advantage of being closer to home. However, we didn't think that company's culture would be a good fit for Megan. Her authentic self is more of a free spirit and the organization she's considering is very strict about dress code and work hours. When we offered this different perspective to Megan, she was quick to respond: *"There's no way someone is going to tell me how I need to dress or be walking the halls at 5:15 p.m. gauging loyalty on the basis of who leaves on time and who stays longer."*

Generation Z cares more about work-life balance and personal well-being than even that of millennials. The model of what work means in the lives of Gen Z and of what work actually *is* appears to be very different for this new group now at the entry level of most organizations. We're finding that balance and well-being are of greater importance to this young generation than income or building a career profile and reputation.

The youngest of this generation are showing even more of this sentiment. A recent survey of 2,000 American high school students found that 82 percent agree that the most important thing to them is to do something they're passionate about, regardless of what career they choose. Over half of students surveyed (55 percent) believe college isn't a requirement for a successful career.[9]

Gen Z are also proving to be the most inclusive and diversity-seeking generation yet, even beyond that of millennials. They're a consensus-building generation and expect a collaborative work environment. Benefits such as paid time off, mental-health days, and work-related activities that create a sense of community are essential to this group.

So, what do these generational dynamics mean in an evolving workplace and how could they best inform your career decisions? It should all begin with how well the organization you are currently working for—or one that you're considering—aligns with your career purpose and desired work-life balance. Whether you're entering the workforce for the first time, considering moving up or out, or staying engaged beyond retirement in a new capacity, there are many options open to you now. Yet, in light of all of these changes, we believe the most promising and fulfilling is the ability to pursue a career with purpose beyond retirement.

Lifelong Reinvention

Earlier, we spoke of how baby boomers are boomeranging back into the workplace and how organizations are encouraging their return. An example of this is in the healthcare industry where many boomer physicians are looking to retire. This coincides with the steadily growing number of boomers retiring in general since 2011, the year the oldest reached age 65.

Yet, healthcare systems are trying to retain retiring physicians primarily to coach and develop the younger doctors and interns coming in; and many are agreeing to stay. They're no longer seeing patients and practicing medicine, but they're staying on nevertheless and working part-time. This is not just happening in healthcare. We're finding many older employees considering returning, renewing their careers, and remaining relevant in the marketplace. Many who are seeking reemployment tell us that they felt forced to retire, but now find themselves in their late 60s and early 70s looking at life and thinking, *"I have an active mind, so much more to offer experientially, and a lot of energy left."*

People's productive years have gone from a very defined, specific time-frame to much more of a broader and varied one, creating a greater need for lifelong learning. This is an expectation on the part of a growing number of boomers that organizations will have to address in their employee development programs. The reality is that lifelong reinvention is going to be with us for all time to come. Longer lifespans will continue to challenge our traditional ideas about careers, retirement, work-life balance, and more. Changes in the way we now view these belief structures are already having an impact on the way we work, the reason we work, what we do when we work, and most important, the meaning of work in our lives.

A key insight for you as you conduct your search for a career with purpose is to make ongoing education a focal point of your career decision-making process. What we're finding is that, during job interviews, people of all generations, especially millennials and Gen Z, are beginning to ask, *"Tell me a little bit about your employee development programs"* and *"How will I be developed for new opportunities?"* and *"Please share some insight into the culture of your company."*

In addition to the changing profile of the American workforce as a factor furthering the evolution of the workplace are the new technologies that are changing the form and nature of work and the ways in which you can participate.

Technology as a Disabler, and Enabler

Another inflection point in this dynamic era is the increased use of automation and artificial intelligence and the birth of human collaboration with robotics. As example, as of the writing of this book, Amazon leads the robotics race in ecommerce and is already transforming the warehouse industry, which today employs more than 1.1 million Americans.[10] In this industry, warehouse bots have the potential to eliminate some of the most menial of warehouse labor, freeing up people to perform more valuable and complex work.

Given their size and dominance, Amazon is an important company to watch in how they create collaborative work environments between humans and robots. Robotics may be on the rise, but Amazon is hiring a lot of humans. In the first ten months of 2020, Amazon added 427,300 employees, bringing its global workforce to more than 1.2 million, up more than 50 percent from the prior year.[11]

The velocity of change is going to increase dramatically and affect most every industry as it looks to bring efficiency and cost-effectiveness to menial and repetitive forms of work. Changes at this magnitude in workforce dynamics typically happen once in a generation, but because of advances in technology, we're experiencing dramatic shifts every couple of years now in how work gets done. We believe this will continue to accelerate as new technologies dissolve old expectations.

The best way to prepare for the disruptive changes that may come to your career through automation, robotics, and AI is to transition yourself away from careers whose work requirements are largely routine and predictable. You need to understand and define your value in the world of work, to recognize the changes and the shifts that are coming, and be prepared with how you're going to position yourself today and five years from now to remain relevant.

Areas of Human Dominance

We see certain areas of work that, for the foreseeable future, will certainly be conducted by humans and may actually be the last bastions of human-dominated work. One such capacity is people-oriented work requiring caring and empathy such as health care providers, therapists, and social workers. This would also include attorneys, consultants, and politicians who work to understand and, in many cases, represent the needs of their clients.

Creative work requiring the conceptualizing or inventing of something new is another area of human uniqueness. The ability to think outside the box in non-linear and non-predictable ways is still an advantage we humans have over artificial intelligence. Another area of human dominance into the foreseeable future is that of skilled-trade workers such as electricians, carpenters, plumbers, and more requiring flexibility and dexterity.

New technologies bringing efficiency and cost-effectiveness to tedious work will certainly separate millions of people from their work over the years to come, yet technological advancements will also enable millions to find new careers by changing the form and nature of the world of work and the ways in which people can participate.

A Borderless Workforce

Many factors over a very short period of time have contributed to freeing people from traditional work constraints and creating much more of an "alternate worker," someone who works on and off campus or completely outside of their organizations. This trend doesn't necessarily apply to those careers and jobs that require an onsite presence such as manufacturing, health care, or hospitality. Nevertheless, there are tens of millions of people today working remotely, 22 percent of the workforce actually, and projections are that the number will increase dramatically in the next few years.[12]

There are many definitions of a borderless workforce. It generally means that companies have begun to allow their employees to have more flexible hours and work remotely—essentially doing business outside the walls of an office or borders of a corporate campus. Companies have also started focusing on team-based models for decision-making versus traditional hierarchical business models. The borders that we used to place internally on functional areas such as accounting, HR, and product development are starting to blur as many workplaces are evolving to new team structures.

One of North America's leading broad-line global suppliers of maintenance, repair, and operating (MRO) products doesn't have a separate HR team assigned to each of its departments as do many traditional companies of their size and nature. They have, instead, a pool of HR personnel who bid to work on projects and come together as work groups to undertake the assignment.

Scrum teams are another example of how the whole philosophy of borders and team structures is changing. Scrum, a term used in rugby to help team members work better together, has grown in popularity among millennials and Generation Z. It encourages teams to learn through experiences, self-organize while working on a problem, and reflect on their wins and losses so as to improve continuously.

The Offer of Well-Being

Another inflection point in the workplace is the shift away from employee engagement to a greater focus on employee well-being. As people are considering the direction of their career and the changing shape and intention of the workplace, it's no longer just about the financial package.

Gallup scientists have been studying Americans' expectations of a life well-lived since the mid-twentieth century. More recently, in partnership with economists, psychologists, and scientists, they have researched the common elements of well-being that transcend countries and cultures: Career Well-Being, Social Well-Being, Financial Well-Being, Physical Well-Being, and Community Well-Being [13] as the following graphic illustrates.

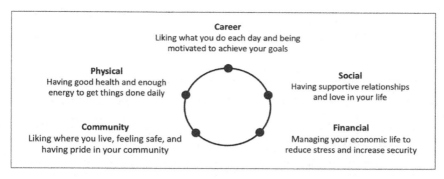

We will come back to the topic of well-being in greater detail later in the book; however, we're highlighting it here because of its influence today in the workplace, especially among millennials and Gen Z. As we illustrated earlier, well-being is significant to the younger generations and they're more vocal about it than their predecessors. Companies are beginning to realize this, as are Gen Xers and boomers who've been influenced by their younger successors and are altering their perceptions and expectations of work-life harmony. A big part of this well-being movement is having greater flexibility in choosing where, how, and when you work.

How Do You Want to Engage?

A workforce study conducted in May and June of 2021 with more than 9,000 American workers found convincing reasons for employers to consider bringing remote workers back to the office in a hybrid fashion, spending part of the work week at home and part on-site.[14] These statistics prove how the workforce has not just evolved but metamorphized in their work preferences in just under two years.

- 91 percent of workers in the U.S. working at least some of their hours remotely are hoping their ability to work at home persists after the pandemic.

- Overall, 54 percent of employees who work remotely at least some of the time say they would ideally like to split their time between working at home and in the office—a hybrid arrangement.

- A little over a third (37 percent) would like to work from home exclusively, while only nine percent want to return to the office full time.

Time preservation is the key reason for wanting to work remotely, specifically for having the flexibility to balance work and personal obligations. Improved well-being by having more time for one's self and to be with one's family were also key reasons for preferring remote work.

In a separate study, 23 percent of Americans surveyed said they would take a 10 percent pay cut to work from home permanently.[15] We read this as a signal of the changing meaning of work in people's lives. Organizations trying to hold onto traditional values and work models will lose out on recruiting and retaining younger employees. We believe that "working structures" centering around how people want to work will be the most sought-after benefit a company can offer.

Self-Awareness as a Job Skill

As we've shared throughout this chapter, there are many changes in just the last couple of years that have unleashed a new and different workplace and workforce. We believe that one of the best job skills that anyone can have in this evolving work world is that of self-awareness. You have to be cognizant of the kind of career you want and for what purpose; how you want to work; and the well-being you want to derive from the one-third of your life that you'll spend working. In essence, if the workplace is evolving at a faster rate than ever before, then you have to be actively engaged and open and resilient to those changes.

Self-awareness begins with understanding your true strengths and weaknesses. Most important is being honest about your weaknesses. Impatience or being a perfectionist may be shrewd things to say in an interview when asked what your weaknesses are. However, those aren't honest weaknesses. Interviewers will want to know your true limitations or challenges such as *"I prefer working alone and not on teams"* or *"I can only be on-site three days a week."*

Don't be reticent about sharing your true weaknesses with recruiters. They may be your preferences really and chances are strong that you'll still get hired, though you may be placed in a different role than you initially would have imagined. Yet it could be a role that may suit your need in the long run. Be open to the fact that companies are going to start looking at their workforce in a much different way by saying, *"Well, I know you've had training in this area, but I think you'd be great in this position."*

Andy's recent career change is a perfect example of how companies are viewing their employees in a new light and it's happening in our own organization of ten people. We just hired Andy, a professional coach and operations specialist, to a sales role here at LAK Group. Andy never sold a day in his life but we see something in him and believe he'll be great at it.

Andy has all of the intangibles. He cares about what he's doing and fits our culture very well. Almost anyone can learn to sell, but to us, learning and believing in our products and services and aligning with our culture are the more important values. Andy's desires and purpose in life to be both a coach and technician will find a home here.

A key takeaway for you in all of this is to assess your strengths and keep your finger on the pulse of the changes that are taking place in the workplace in general and in your industry. Apply what you've learned in this chapter to develop more of a three-dimensional view of your current environment and future as you work at defining and securing a career with purpose.

Careers Are Evolving

This chapter has been all about the workplace evolving around us, but as in every ecosystem, all elements must evolve together, including you. It's difficult to say if colleges are going to catch onto this or not, but young people today need to develop within themselves a sort of sentinel: a consciousness of their character, feelings, and purpose—an ever-vigilant awareness of themselves and of the changing workplace landscape.

Maintaining that kind of consciousness is not an easy task. Many people fall onto a career track and ride it for years, even decades, only to find they've lost their sense of purpose, or their occupation has evolved past them or dissolved completely at the hands of technology. If they adopt the perspective that their careers are also part of that evolutionary process that reshapes, morphs, and changes, they too will grow and advance within that shifting environment.

In our career development practice, we help people seeking or facing a transition in their careers to learn the concept of mental agility; of being adaptable, moment-to-moment, and learning to apply new insights in a very short period of time. Colleges may not yet be teaching career evolution but we are. The workplace has and will always evolve, yet it feels as if the wheels of change are spinning much faster in recent years. In many ways, they certainly are. As you're evaluating your career, your ability to comprehend these changes and be adaptable is a critical skill that you will need going forward.

Questions to Reflect On

1. How do you evaluate the way the marketplace and the direction the industry that you're interested in is evolving? In what ways do these changes work for or against your best interests?

2. As you think about your career and where you want to work, how important is flexibility in terms of place (office/hybrid/remote) and time (work hours)?

3. What kind of environment do you like to work in? Do you prefer working on teams or working alone? Do you require supervision or prefer autonomy?

4. What are your non-negotiables when considering a company? What are the things you will not do or will not do without as you evaluate companies?

5. What aspects of an organization are essential to you, such as its diversity, employee development programs, well-being programs, or flexible working arrangements? Which of these is most important? Are there other considerations of greater importance?

6. Is a company's culture important to you? If so, what values and behaviors are most important? What are least important?

4

Traditional Career Paths Won't Work

"Almost every significant breakthrough is the result of a courageous break with traditional ways of thinking."
—Stephen Covey

Becky is overcome with both joy and sadness as she reads and rereads the offer from the company she interviewed with two weeks ago. The joy in her heart comes from knowing she nailed the interview and that this means a job with great pay, great benefits, and the promise of a career. The sadness is in realizing that by accepting their offer, she'll have to move to the other side of the country, time zones away from her family and childhood friends. Her gloom also comes from a feeling that the decision has already been made for her.

Since high school, Becky's father has encouraged her to *"get in with a company, work hard, and move up."* She knows that if she turns this offer down, her dad will be very disappointed in her, a thought that now overrides all of her other considerations. Yet, what gives Becky the greatest anxiety is the feeling deep inside that the industry and career she's entering don't genuinely reflect her true ambitions.

Stories such as Becky's are increasingly common today. In our evolving workplace, people, especially those of the younger generations, are questioning and breaking away from the traditional concept of work. Instead, they're looking for greater work-life balance, with an emphasis on meaningful careers and more personal time. We're finding that this change in thinking about the meaning and value of work is also challenging our long-standing attitudes about career paths and career ladders.

Our intent in this chapter is to help you gain a new perspective on what a career path can be in today's evolving workplace. We also provide you the tools to ensure the path you take is centered on your needs and aspirations.

All four generations working today have been conditioned to think and act along the lines of traditionally vertical paths. Even Gen Z now entering the workplace, like Becky in the story above, are choosing or being directed by family, managers, and even HR departments toward the first rungs of their career ladders. How do you know if your ladder is on the right wall to begin with? Let's begin working from there.

Career Portfolio vs Path

Creating a career portfolio (or work portfolio) rather than a career path is how people are viewing their careers today. They're collecting experiences as they move from one role to another in their company, or change companies, or jump into completely different industries. They're not following career paths assigned to them by their employers but rather finding their own way and, as a result, creating a portfolio of experiences filled with meaningful work that *they* have chosen for themselves.

An increasing number of companies are participating in this trend, accelerated by millennials and Generation Z—those from their 40s to their early 20s. Organizations have embraced it by placing greater value on developing their employees and hiring new talent with diverse experiential backgrounds. Employers are assessing skills on a resume differently than in the past (we'll cover that in the next chapter) and finding that by getting behind this new orientation, they're able to retain their talent, develop them, and advance them in their careers.

So, what's your next move? It could be successive or sideways. It could be to a different functional area within your company or to an altogether different company or industry. In our practice, we're coming across more and more professionals, from boomers to millennials, changing careers in midstream. We see people in operations and finance taking up human resource management positions, engineers becoming salespeople, IT specialists moving into marketing, teachers finding corporate roles, and healthcare professionals shifting into law enforcement.

We are also experiencing a movement of professionals into new and different industries including manufacturing professionals into healthcare, profit into non-profit segments, corporate roles into small business owner-ship and interesting trends to owning and operating franchises.

The best way to begin thinking about your next step is to first come to terms with your true aspirations—your hopes and ambitions for achieving something. Then it's knowing the skills and experiences you'll need to fulfill your career goals. It may be through your careful search of organizations that suit your needs or the path of self-employment that can help give you the experiences to master those skills.

To that end, the focus of this chapter will be on how to think in terms of a career portfolio instead of a traditional career path, how to build a career portfolio, and ways you can navigate this evolving workplace with openness and flexibility. First things first.

It's Less about Loyalty

Young and inexperienced persons often can be remarkably wise. That was Mike Milsted's first thought as he reflected back on his conversation with his nine-year-old daughter Ella years ago. It was she who tipped the scales in helping him decide to leave his company after 15 years. Her simple questions on why he was there, for what must have seemed like an eternity to her, were a breakthrough for him.

He thought to himself, *"What does 'length of employment' really mean as a value to me other than I can run a marathon? What did I learn in that timeframe? How have I grown in my experiences?"* He needed to do something that was dramatically different, something that was more aligned with his own personal mission statement of what he wanted to be, where he wanted to be, and what he wanted to do. It was at that moment that Mike realized he needed to make a change, if for anything, as a statement to himself.

Fifteen or more years at a company would be considered a mark of loy-alty in anyone's book, but because of his daughter's innocent line of inquiry, Mike began to see his career as less about being loyal to someone or some-thing else and more about being faithful to himself.

In your pursuit of a career with purpose, make sure that your efforts are closely aligned with what it is that *you* want to accomplish. It's often just a matter of letting go of the security blanket of having to climb a ladder up a wall prescribed to you and instead taking measures into your own hands. Your professional growth and development and the experiences you gain throughout your work life need not follow a straight path.

Careers Are No Longer Linear

Traditional career paths simply don't work well in meeting the preferences of people in today's evolving marketplace. Think of the conventional career path as a map that says you start at position **A**, then move up to **B**, then climb to **C**, after a number of years and sufficient dues have been paid. Get in the ground floor with a company, and your future is predestined in terms of what your role will be and what you'll be groomed to become.

We don't believe that there needs to be a beginning or ending point to a career with predetermined rungs on a ladder. For many people today, a career journey has more to do with self-discovery than it does advancement.

Let's look at the traditional ways companies view career paths. At a very high level of differentiation, organizations tend to leverage either a ladder or lattice approach to careers. Simply put, career ladders are vertical rungs, progressions of roles or career steps that move you upward in an organization, as depicted by the graphic on the left.

Career lattices are represented by the graphic on the right with pathways that can take your career in either horizontal or vertical directions within an organization. In companies that offer career lattices, you don't have to remain in a functional area or department in order to grow and advance.

Career Ladders   **Career Lattices**

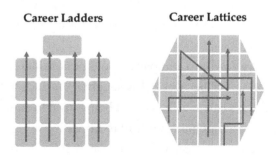

Career ladders are a traditional framework that shows the specific sequence of job positions a person should progress through in order to reach a more senior level with more responsibility, higher pay, and greater benefits. Career lattices, on the other hand, offer alternatives for growth and development with more flexible plans that support employee development and upskilling in multiple directions, or the opportunity to remain in a position longer than prescribed.

It is true that well-defined career ladders can still work very well for some organizations and for some individuals. Using visuals to communicate to employees a specific upward progression to senior positions makes sense. It provides encouragement and the realization that hard work and loyalty will pay off in the long run.

However, we believe this can potentially close the door on many opportunities for you as an individual serving your own purpose. It also potentially closes doors for the company by not allowing you to develop and apply your natural talents and skills. Moreover, you could be waiting forever for your manager or human resources department to help you plan and achieve your next career move.

Below is an example of a traditional career ladder in the field of healthcare.[16] Many in this industry tell us that they find their career paths confusing and limiting in opportunity and exploration of interests. It indicates to them that they can only go down one path such as pharmacy, radiology, or dental. What if they want to start as a certified nursing assistant, spend time in a lab as they get their biology degree, scribe for a physician, and then go to medical school to become a nurse, case worker, or physician themselves? How do assigned paths help them connect to those experiences?

We spent a great deal of time working with organizations on building career paths, and in each instance without fail, the projects always come to a screeching halt because the pathways become far too complicated. When we work with an organization's job descriptions, we create graphs that have various positions with arrows leading to different roles. Each time, without fail, we end up with a conference room wall filled with poster paper and whiteboard outlines of the routes that different jobs could feed into.

Healthcare Career Paths

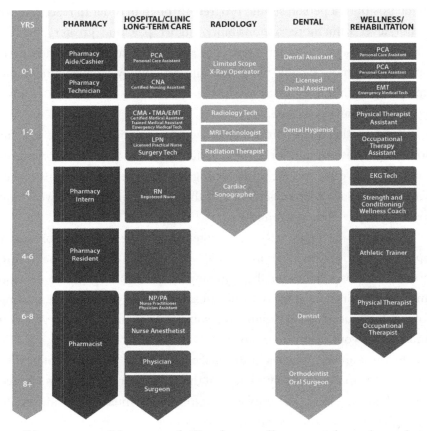

YRS	PHARMACY	HOSPITAL/CLINIC LONG-TERM CARE	RADIOLOGY	DENTAL	WELLNESS/ REHABILITATION
0-1	Pharmacy Aide/Cashier	PCA Personal Care Assistant	Limited Scope X-Ray Operaator	Dental Assistant	PCA Personal Care Assistant
	Pharmacy Technician	CNA Certified Nursing Assistant		Licensed Dental Assistant	PCA Personal Care Assistant
					EMT Emergency Medical Tech
1-2		CMA · TMA/EMT Certified Medical Assistant Trained Medical Assistant Emergency Medical Tech	Radiology Tech	Dental Hygienist	Physical Therapist Assistant
		LPN Licensed Practical Nurse	MRI Technologist		Occupational Therapy Assistant
		Surgery Tech	Radiation Therapist		
4	Pharmacy Intern	RN Registered Nurse	Cardiac Sonographer		EKG Tech
					Strength and Conditioning/ Wellness Coach
4-6	Pharmacy Resident				Athletic Trainer
6-8		NP/PA Nurse Practitioner Physician Assistant		Dentist	Physical Therapist
		Nurse Anesthetist			Occupational Therapist
	Pharmacist				
8+		Physician		Orthodontist Oral Surgeon	
		Surgeon			

It's a non-sensible approach. Fundamentally, every job at a lower level can be a feeder position to every job at the next level up; and the same for the next level after that. Trying to map those progressions is often a frustrating and ultimately fruitless exercise, yet there are many companies that still do it this way. But as you'll discover, not all are following this traditional model. This is why we suggested in the last chapter that you ask your company, or the ones that you're interested in joining, to share with you their approach to employee development and what kinds of programs they offer. That's an immediate sign for you about where their focus lies.

As you go about assessing companies in your pursuit of a career with purpose, realize that the traditional ways in which organizations have approached career pathing is changing. It's no longer strictly vertical and up. Your career can take any direction. Don't limit yourself by thinking about it from the standpoint of, as example, becoming a financial analyst, then a manager of a team of analysts, then eventually director or VP of finance.

Think more along the lines of things you want to achieve in that one-third of your life spent working at something. That's the path that will benefit you the most and, in the long run, bring you the greatest personal fulfillment. It may not be an upward rung or even staying in the same field. It may be a downward step in order to move up in another direction. You may want to shift from finance to marketing so you can build the broader experiences you'll need to be a division manager for that company, or to start your own business in ten years. Seek out companies that will allow you to build a career portfolio that meets your needs and helps you develop the skills and experiences that are important and have meaning to you.

One of the largest financial services firms in the U.S. has had in place for the past twenty years a rotational job program that gives their up-and-coming leaders the opportunity to work in different functional areas of the company such as accounts payable, client relations, or human resource management. The company's intention is to help their employees build a portfolio of experiences and discover and develop their talents and skills. It's self-serving as well.

The program has been a tremendous boon to the company. Their retention rates are some of the highest in the industry. Moreover, years of cross-training their employee population has developed a pool of individuals with a broad and deep understanding of the many facets of their company and not just that of their own department or division.

People want to broaden their horizons, grow in their careers, and excel in new challenges. Companies are beginning to understand this and helping their employees navigate their careers. Be prepared for this trend from ladder to lattice. Rather than create a career path for yourself, your goal should be to create a career portfolio, and as you go through this process, center your attention and energy on what direction you want your work life to go and then target those organizations that can best support your ambitions.

Building Your Career Portfolio

For many of us, every three to five years sets off an internal radar that signals us to do something with our careers. Since our work consumes such
a huge percentage of our lives and deeply affects our well-being, it's not
surprising that what we do for a living is so important to us. Nowadays,
expanding one's career is seen as normal, even expected, behavior. In fact,
many employers assume that the majority of the people on their teams
have their radars engaged at all times.

While a career path tends to reflect a linear track in a specific skill, a
career portfolio can represent a vast and diverse personal and professional
journey. It should include all the various twists and turns that have shaped
your work life and even personal life.

For those just starting their career journey, don't expect to have everything mapped out all the way through to a destination. Center your attention instead on your purpose and aspirations. This will automatically allow
more opportunities to surface from your self-reflection. Additionally, your
career portfolio doesn't have to be limited to traditional paid jobs. If you
were a lifeguard during your high school years, or serve on a school board,
or help as a community volunteer, or if you have a hobby that you're especially good at, include those in your portfolio. Employers today are looking
to hire talent with non-traditional backgrounds and your career portfolio
can make the connection for them.

For example, Rosetta's advanced degree in college was in world history, a topic she loved dearly having been a "military brat" growing up in
both Asia and Europe. Her ultimate dream was to teach history, though life
doesn't always follow the path we create for ourselves. So, Rosetta began
selling life insurance and became very successful at building and sustaining client relationships.

Today she works for one of the largest automobile manufacturers as a
cultural advisor to their international teams. Her knowledge of world history,
having lived in different countries, and her client relationship skills make her
a uniquely qualified treasure for her company. Rosetta loves her work and is
fulfilling her ultimate dream, although in a most unexpected way.

What Are *Your* Career Aspirations?

What is the role of work in your life beyond just making money or paying your mortgage or making rent, paying for your car and lifestyle, or creating a college fund for your children? The first step in building a career portfolio is to reflect on what's most important to you, but don't think in terms of paths or ladders or financial responsibilities.

For this moment, set all those considerations aside and think only in terms of your career aspirations—your hopes or ambitions for achieving something meaningful in your life. Go back as far as you like: to college or even high school.

Part of this reflection is to examine your beliefs about who you are. We often find that the career path people are on has a direct relationship to the stories they've been told to believe all their lives about who they are, whether by their parents, teachers, or managers at work.

Brian is in the middle of his career and now finds himself in outplacement after devoting 17 years to one company. His new boss, who's been on the job for three months and upon assessing her team, decided to downsize Brian.

Although Brian is highly intelligent and very capable, creative, and productive in his role, he has a few personality quirks that, at times, make it difficult for his teammates to understand him. Rather than taking the time to determine how she could develop Brian given all his other attributes and knowledge of the company, she decided to let him go. The reason she gave him was, *"You're a great analyst, but I can read people and know their potential, and you'll never be a leader. There's no one better at what you do as an analyst, but I need someone that can lead the group."*

In the process of our helping Brian find his next job, a company offered him a management position over their analytics department. He shared his news with us but with an uneasiness and uncertainty.

He began by telling us, *"I applied for an analyst position but they're looking for someone to lead the team. I can't do that. I don't know that I want to do that."*

We asked, *"Why do you believe that this is something that you don't think you can do? Or is it that you don't have an interest in leading people?"*

Brian replies without hesitation, *"Oh no, I love working with people, and I love to help them develop and understand how to ask questions and how to get to the right answers."*

"So, you like to coach other people and mentor them?"

"Yes," he said.

"Then why can't you see yourself managing and leading people?" we asked.

Brian then went into his story about what his last boss said about him not being leadership material and his finding greater success in the marketplace if he remained an analyst. As a result, Brian had based his entire search on an analyst's position with no positive responses until this one opportunity, but as a manager of analysts.

Many people come to us who've been told stories of who they are, what they're capable of, and what they're destined to become. We find they're told these things at any stage of their lives—as children, teens, or adults—and it becomes their self-fulfilling prophecy. We find a direct correlation between the stories that people are told and the careers they choose for themselves.

As we shared in Chapter 1, in order to find a career with meaning that will sustain your needs and desires, you have to address the stories that you've chosen to believe about who you are, what your value is, and what you're capable of doing. It's ultimately *you* who gets to choose those stories and the kind of career that will bring you satisfaction and happiness.

The Well-Being of Your Career

In Chapter 2, we shared how millennials, and even more so, Gen Z, are more intent on finding work-life balance and personal well-being than any past generation in recent history. When we think of well-being as a pursuit, we think of *Gallup's National Health and Well-Being Index*, which measures Americans' perceptions of their lives and their daily experiences. In their research, they identified five interrelated elements that make up personal well-being: a sense of purpose, social relationships, financial security, relationship to community, and physical health.[17]

We believe Gallup offers one of the more comprehensive studies on well-being and find that their model provides a comprehensive framework for evaluating your career and what's most important to you from an overall well-being perspective, what we term Career Well-Being. Just as in your quest for personal well-being, your ultimate goal in this context is to find balance and personal satisfaction across all five aspects of your career.

Career Well-Being

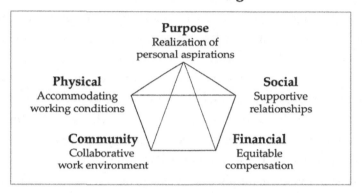

Let's deep dive into each of these elements and measure the health and happiness of your career. As you reflect on the status and expectations of each, keep in mind that all five should be considered equally valuable to create a well-balanced career and life. As example, although money is important, Financial cannot have more value than Purpose, nor should Social without a balanced consideration for income override Financial or any of the other elements.

In terms of your sense of **Purpose**, do you enjoy your work? Do you rise out of bed each morning with drive and energy, already formulating your plans for the day? Purpose is the first measure of well-being in a career. It's about knowing what you want to achieve ultimately. You certainly want to be active in your career, but there's a difference between activity and productivity. You want to be running in a race toward something. You need to know what your goal is, and that goal has to be something that gives you energy.

Social is the quality of having supportive relationships. It also speaks to the type of person you are and what you value. Close relationships can be critical to the security and comfort you feel as you pursue your career. Does your family give you positive energy every day? Do they show enthusiasm in your career and what you've accomplished? Do you have friends who are supportive of you and act as trusted sounding boards for your ideas?

Your social well-being at work can be just as critical to your overall career well-being. Do you find your company's culture and your co-workers positive and stimulating? It's also common for people to prefer working independently and not work in team environments. In those instances, their social well-being is found in their freedom to work independently.

When it comes to **Financial**, be mindful not to put too much weight on how much you're making in lieu of the other elements. Financial is an important consideration, but your goal is to keep all five essentials in balance. Having said that, you want to make sure that your career is able to support you and your family and that you're doing a job that pays you fairly. However, there are other values aside from salary that translate to monetary gain.

Ask yourself: what has the same value of money to you? Having workplace flexibility as example indirectly increases your net gain because you're not commuting to work every day, thereby reducing fuel costs and wear and tear on your vehicle. You're also lowering your cost for automobile insurance, dry cleaning, lunch, and other expenses that add up.

Community is an element of well-being that comes from working on teams collaboratively, sharing ideas and learning together, and being able to influence others in an organization. It's a feeling of belonging that can also extend to the products and services produced by your company that support your purpose and align with your values.

Physical well-being is you having the choice about where you work, when you work, and how you work. Physical speaks to the bodily demands of the job. Teaching, as example, requires standing on your feet most of the day, or your job may require sitting in front of a computer screen all day, or talking with customers on the phone. Physical is also the traveled distance to and from work.

All generations today are more intent on finding greater work-life balance. We believe the pandemic that forced so many of us to work from home and rearrange all aspects of our lives to accommodate that change has enlightened us and forced us to find a way. In a way, the genie is out of the bottle. Now, many of us who have found that balance want to maintain it for the well-being of our personal lives. This change has also encouraged us to focus on and improve the well-being of our careers.

To that end, your ultimate goal is to maintain balance among the five elements of career well-being: knowing your purpose and what you want to achieve ultimately in your career, having supportive relationships at home and at work, being paid a fair compensation, feeling a sense of community and belonging, and benefiting from accommodating working conditions.

Approach with Openness and Flexibility

Much has changed in the workplace in just the last couple of years, all of which has been considerably affected, and in many ways accelerated, by the pandemic. A new generation of leadership in the C-suite of every industry is bringing a unique perspective to workplace structures and collaborative cultures. More than ever before, younger generations are pursuing working lives that conform to their personal lives and are encouraging organizations to step up and offer employee development and flexible work arrangements. Even the attitudes of boomers are changing with many seeking second, more meaningful careers—reentering instead of retiring.

In addition to generational dynamics, the pace of change driven by technology will continue to affect every industry as companies, pursuing greater efficiencies, shift menial and repetitive forms of work to automation and robotics. As we shared earlier, change of this magnitude in workforce dynamics typically occurs once in a generation, but because of advances in technology, these shifts are occurring more often.

We often recommend books for our clients from authors whose perspectives align with our own. April Rinne's book, *Flux: 8 Superpowers for*

Thriving in Constant Change, notes that the pace of change has never been as fast as it is today, and yet, is likely to never again be this slow. [18]

Rinne gives the example that the effects of the First Industrial Revolution took several generations to be fully felt, while today's Fourth Industrial Revolution will take a fraction of that time. It's an interesting concept because so many of us believe that things are changing too fast already. The author goes on to define the eight flux superpowers that can keep you grounded when the ground beneath you is shifting:

- Running slower
- Seeing what's invisible
- Getting lost
- Starting with trust
- Knowing that you're "enough"
- Creating your portfolio career
- Being all the more human
- Letting go of the future

A world in "flux" calls for a new mindset, one that treats constant change and uncertainty as features of life. Find and keep your focus as you pursue your search for a career with purpose. Set aside the weight and frustration of the unknown and shift your energy and attention toward the well-being of your career.

Career paths can take many different shapes and directions in today's evolving workplace. Your professional growth and development and the experiences you gain throughout your work life need not follow a straight path any longer. Be open to change and flexible in how you adapt to new circumstances as they arise. Ensure that the path you take is centered on your needs and aspirations. Once you know your own value and know your purpose and story, you're ready to write your resume.

Questions to Reflect On

1. What is one of the stories you've chosen to believe about who you are?

2. What impact do you want to be able to make through your work and are you able to have that impact where you are now?

3. Do you look at your experiences as random independent events? Or are they all linked in some common way that has allowed you to create a career path that's unique to who you are? What are those links?

4. How have you prepared thus far for the speed of change? What will you do differently, if anything, in the next year or two?

5. In your career, what's the difference between getting things done and having a meaningful impact?

6. Does your career search satisfy career well-being for yourself?

5

Telling Your Story

"There have been great societies that did not use the wheel,
but there have been no societies that did not tell stories."
—Ursula K. Le Guin

In 1482, at the age of 30, Leonardo da Vinci wrote a letter listing his capabilities and accomplishments and sent it to the Duke of Milan to gain his sponsorship for a job. Although da Vinci was already known for his artistic abilities, his letter instead focused on his aptitude for making covered chariots safe and unattackable, a known need of the Duke at the time. You see, before he was famous as an artist at an even younger age, Leonardo was a craftsman, a carpenter of sorts who made devices and machines.

Da Vinci had already made impressive contributions to the art world, but those were excluded from his list of accomplishments because they weren't relevant to the Duke's needs. Instead, da Vinci's letter, which is now credited as being the first "resume" ever recorded, focused on what his target audience was most interested in at the time, covered chariots, and got him the commission.

What made da Vinci's resume so effective and still talked about even today was in how personalized it was. It wasn't simply a cataloging of his talents and skills as an artist. Rather, the story Leonardo chose to tell in that document and in his interview with the Duke communicated strengths and accomplishments highly tailored to the needs of his audience.

The Power of Storytelling

Storytelling has been a part of how we have communicated and shared our history since the first cave drawings. Communication seems to be part of our DNA. We're confident that if da Vinci had Internet, video, and audio in his time, he would have included, along with his resume, other social media tools such as a LinkedIn profile and website with video clips illustrating his devices in action.

The ability to paint a picture through the use of words, to draw upon the human emotion, and to involve and connect deeply with people is all done through storytelling. Stories promote a common language that bonds us together and enables us to relate to each other in a more meaningful way.

Storytelling also helps to change our perceptions of ourselves. Developing our stories and linking our experiences and accomplishments to our capabilities often reveals to us those talents we forgot we had, never knew we had, or gave less significance to over the course of our lives. The process of storytelling empowers us and the stories themselves give us confidence. Most important, they guide us toward the careers that could bring us the most joy and satisfaction.

Our goal in this chapter is to help you discover how to use storytelling to unearth in you the talents and skills that you can and should build a meaningful career around. Additionally, you'll learn how to match and communicate your strengths to the needs of the organizations in your marketplace through your resume and supportive social media platforms.

So, What's *Your* Story?

In order for you to reap the power of storytelling, you must first be able to know your backstory: the events and experiences that led up to the person you are today, the talents and skills that you developed along the way, and the value of your accomplishments. Your backstory is about your life's journey to this moment in time and what makes you special. Here's an example of what we mean.

Marie is a single mom who didn't have a car and rode the bus to both take her children to school and herself to work each day. Then, every weekday evening after dinner, she would drop the little ones off at her mother's home and take the metro to the university where she took evening classes. Marie did this for 14 years to achieve her degree. It's a powerful story of grit and determination. Who wouldn't want someone of that caliber on their team?

We often find when helping clients with their own storytelling that they tend to disregard the value of sharing stories of adversity with us as Marie had. They believe that their personal experiences and interests may be irrelevant, even naïve to share, and not qualify them for the role they're hoping to fill. We believe your personal experiences are appropriate if they speak to your natural talents and skills you've honed over time; those things that truly define you and what you'd love to work at each day.

It's all in how you, first, unearth and interpret your strengths. The challenge then becomes communicating those personal aspects of your backstory in your resume while conforming to the content and format expectations of recruiters and hiring managers.

How do you help your audience learn about who you really are and where your strengths and passions lie given the constraints of resume writing? One answer is that you're no longer limited to the confines of a resume to tell your story. You now have social media outlets that you could include with your digital online brand such as a LinkedIn profile, a personal website, YouTube video clips, and so on. The other answer is to view your resume as your calling card and the introduction to your story. Its purpose then becomes twofold: to get the interview, and to provide details that can guide the recruiter or hiring manager to the questions you want them to ask of you.

For instance, Marie doesn't have to mention in her resume about being a single mom and mass transit as her only means of transportation. That kind of personal information is not typically expected in a resume. We did suggest though that Marie add to her education section that she "attended night school while working full time to achieve her degree." That generated the kinds of questions Marie wanted to answer because they revealed her strongest attributes and her passion to succeed.

Here's another example. Steve was a senior vice president of manufacturing, quite advanced in age, and concerned about finding a new job in another industry. When we met Steve, we found that he wasn't gaining much ground with his current autobiography. Through our inquiry process (you'll find this exercise at the end of this chapter), we discovered that Steve was a potato farmer and even grew up on a potato farm. We added that fact as additional employment on his resume— "a lifelong potato farmer who grew up and worked on a family farm."

We also discovered that he raised three Eagle Scouts and was still involved in Scouting. We added those storylines to his community activities section. And so as not to leave anything out that could generate the kinds of questions that Steve would love to answer, we also included in his community section that for the past ten years he had been president of his church's successful summer festivals. He then punctuated his distinctive document with his personal email address, stevethepotatofarmer@gmail.com, in the contact line.

Using his new resume and updated LinkedIn profile, Steve applied for a vice president of manufacturing position in the industry of most interest to him and received a call the very next day. The first thing the hiring manager asked about was Steve's email address, the first thing that caught the manager's eye, enabling Steve to tell the story of his being a potato farmer and having grown up on a family farm, highlighting a work ethic that he established at a young age.

That got him an interview the next day with the president of the company, who began his conversation with Steve asking about Eagle Scouts and getting Steve's thoughts on his son's Eagle project. The president then asked Steve about the success of his parish's summer festivals. They eventually got around to talking about the job itself.

It wasn't until we added well-worded elements of Steve's backstory to his resume that he started generating attention. He received a job offer from the company and established a personal connection and relationship with the president on day one.

The personal information we added was a bit out of the norm for the resume of a vice president of manufacturing, but at the same time, farming and community service were such important elements that defined who Steve was. The way he saw it, if a company rejects him for those kinds of activities, it would not have been a good fit for him in the long run.

There are many facets of yourself that could emerge from your backstory examination. We shared a story in Chapter 4 about Brian, who was told by his new manager, while in the process of laying Brian off, that he wasn't leadership material and that he should focus his efforts on looking for another analyst position. His manager misguided Brian in his job search and put him on the wrong trajectory, and his resume reflected it.

Yet, through our inquiry process, we discovered Brian's passion and talent in leading others. We should say *he* discovered his ability, which caused him to reevaluate his strengths and the way in which he was promoting himself to the marketplace. As a result, Brian was offered a leadership opportunity with a company and a new course for his career. He mustered the courage to interview and win that position because of the leadership talents he discovered in himself and was able to express with confidence.

In Brian's case, he was honest about how he shared his story and was consistent and authentic in his messaging. We believe that the opportunity found Brian and he completed the process by showing up as an authentic person speaking from the heart about what he had done and is capable of doing as a leader. Imagine if Brian had taken the advice of the new manager. He would most likely still be telling her story about himself and the leadership position would never have found him.

The stories we shared about Marie, Steve, and Brian all involved a process of self-discovery that uncovered the talents and skills most meaningful to them and most valuable to their careers. Many people come to us pressured to find their next job or a new career and want to have their updated resume in circulation as quickly as possible.

We believe that in order to find the greatest success in the long run, you shouldn't start writing your resume until you've first determined your talents and skills that best reflect your passions and aptitudes—those which you'd love to build your career around. Before we delve into that self-discovery process, let's first more closely examine what is still the preferred biographical summation of someone seeking employment.

The Evolution of the Resume

Resumes have gone through several updates in terms of formatting, style, and language since the first one was penned by da Vinci more than 500 years ago. They've also been supplemented with social media, personal websites, video bios, and infographics. Yet, employers are still expecting to receive that one document summarizing your accomplishments and highlighting your talents and skills—the resume itself. For that reason, its general format and purpose have remained relatively unchanged.

We're finding that even the younger generations have already been conditioned to conform to standard resume practices. That mindset has even permeated newer social media platforms as well. Scan the countless "About" sections on LinkedIn and you'll find them all pretty much worded the same. If you've read one engineer's or accountant's or marketer's profile summary you've read them all—years of experience in their field and a list of accomplishments and skills.

Over the course of time, we've been habituated to tell our stories as a series of work experiences, bulletizing our responsibilities and accomplishments. This has become the accepted norm and extent of our stories—highly sanitized, abridged, and stylized versions of who we are, yet with care not to include personal information.

There's also a lot of judgment and self-limiting of one's story in order to fit it into the format of a resume. Moreover, many people are so afraid of being judged that they'll withhold significant aspects of who they are regardless of what platform they use. For these reasons, the resume doesn't present itself as a good device for storytelling but more valuable as a calling card to, as we said earlier, elicit a conversation and prompt the interviewer to ask specific questions.

The resume should never be a list of responsibilities. It should speak briefly to your accomplishments and the results of your contributions—proof-points of your value and evidence that the story you're telling about yourself is true.

It should be a thoughtfully crafted document highlighting your strengths as solutions to the organization's challenges and goals, much the same way da Vinci chose to highlight his mechanical versus artistic skills.

The challenge is the resume document itself. How do you get a black-and-white artifact to stand out and tell a compelling story that will help a recruiter or hiring manager immediately grasp what the possibilities may be for you in their company? There isn't a lot of time either to make that impact. Eye tracking studies show that the average initial screening time for a candidate's resume by recruiters and hiring managers is just 7.4 seconds with the majority of those precious moments on the summary statement itself.[19]

Before & After Personal Summaries

We believe it all comes down to the summary statement, the culmination and refinement of your entire story into one short paragraph at the top of your resume with well-chosen and carefully worded proof-points of evidence of your story's authenticity. Here are a few before and after examples of summary statements that made quite a difference in each individual's ability to find meaningful work that aligned more closely with their strengths and interests.

Lauren learned that by using more substantive adjectives, such as "customer-centric" versus "proven and successful," and being brief and more direct in her sentences, she was able to include more detailed language around her skills and accomplishments as a product leader. Additionally, mentioning her emotionally intelligent tendencies and being licensed as a Certified Public Accountant really made her resume stand apart from other product leaders.

Before

Proven and successful product leader with over 30 years of experience building and implementing products, managing customer relationships and driving team enthusiasm. I am passionate about creating products that solve business problems, allowing customers to work more efficiently. My unique skill set combines product leadership, system implementation expertise and accounting experience allowing me to consistently bring new products successfully to market.

After

Customer-centric product leader who creates revenue streams, increases profitability, and grows market share through digital product management and innovation. CEO-minded, applies business acumen, financial strategy and P&L management to achieving business goals. Accomplished in scrum framework, including certifications as Professional Scrum Master and Professional Scrum Product Owner. Leverages foundational field experience and Emotional Intelligence to lead engaged teams, uncover needs, and develop solutions for customers. Certified Public Accountant, State of Wisconsin.

David had an impressive resume filled with skills and accomplishments, but his "before" summary read like a string of cliches and keywords. His "after" summary included more detail on select items relevant to the hiring organizations and use of phrasing as evidence of his experience and accomplishments. David's brief listing of specific skills of most interest to him and those that he would like to develop further says far more than empty statements such as, "understands the big picture."

Before

Seasoned and performance-driven leader with strong commercial acumen and extensive experience in directing end-to-end recruitment process, standardizing performance management practices, and driving crucial staffing decisions. Involved in all HR functions, building and re-staffing organizations, overhauling recruiting standards, and restructuring benefits programs. A problem-solver with ability to understand the big picture, envision solutions, and execute with ease across all organizational levels.

After

Innovative, collaborative Human Resources leader known for defining, developing, and implementing strategic and tactical HR initiatives to support both daily operations and long-range corporate initiatives. Solid business acumen and pragmatism, effectively balancing business issues with employee advocacy. Develops organizational design and restructuring plans to optimize resource allocation. Key advisor and hands-on coach to business leadership, HR team and line management. Transforms organizations with focus on talent acquisition and retention, diverse leadership pipeline, succession planning, performance management and driving engagement.

Brian's inquiry process helped him discover that he was more than just another "marketing professional." We found there were specific industry experiences all of which he would enjoy working in and diverse experiences as well that reflected his deepest interests. His summary changed to echo those more detailed storylines.

Before

Strategic marketing professional with more than fifteen years of experience in market research, brand licensing, and sales support. Energetic self-starter possessing strong communication, project management, analytical and cross-functional team-building skills with competencies in:

After

Marketing and Consumer Insights Manager with MBA and expertise in project scoping, planning, and ideation. Identifies, leverages, and synthesizes information from diverse resources. Creates insightful presentations with clear and compelling insights that enable key stakeholders through informed decision-making. Experience in specialty vehicle/automotive manufacturing, consumer durable products, management consulting, electric and gas utilities, and financial services. Competencies include:

Carlos rewrote his summary statement to position himself first as a strategic business leader and second as an HR professional. He also discovered that he could include more examples of skills and involvements in his summary statement by not taking up word space by mentioning the number of years in HR or the types of industries that he worked in.

Before

Human Resource Professional with over 20 years of leadership experience that spans across non-profit healthcare, professional services, and global manufacturing. Background in organizational change, mergers and acquisitions, building and growing synchronized operating teams, and implementing progressive and innovative practices in high-growth organizations.

After

Innovative and strategic business leader partnering across the organization to scale growth and expansion through cultural transformation, organizational design, and HR leadership. Achieves "employer of choice" brand through cost savings from benefits design and administration, retention of top talent, and organizational efficiencies. Workforce strategist who increases organizational agility and sustainability through performance management, leadership development, and alignment.

The resume may have a different tone and format than other social media platforms and there are norms that make it a bit more challenging for storytelling, yet it still serves a significant purpose. It's your calling card designed to get the interview. It frames what your story is about and lets your other media—your LinkedIn profile, your own personal website, whatever you choose—color in that framework to indicate to recruiting and hiring managers the depth and dimension of who you are.

Many people like to say that *"the best indicator of the future is through past results."* We frankly believe it's your ability to tell your story about what you've done that serves as the best gauge of your future capabilities and accomplishments. You may be the smartest person in the world, but if you can't tell your story and what it means for the hiring organization, you'll find it increasingly difficult to get the job or enter the career you're really hoping for that will have the most meaning and be the most satisfying to you.

Your Mindset, Skillset, and Toolset

Now that we discussed the resume and its importance as the introduction to your story, let's now focus on identifying the talents and skills that you would love to build a career around by appraising (1) your mindset and how you view your natural and learned capabilities; (2) your skillset, the talents and skills that build to your strengths; and (3) and your toolset, the methods you will use to convey your story to the marketplace.

Your Mindset: *Owning Your Light*

Begin your process by looking inward. What are the stories that you've chosen to believe or not believe over the course of your life and career about who you are and what you're capable of? Is your career really yours, or is it someone else's interpretation of what it should be?

Recognizing and releasing yourself of the constraints of others' expectations of you, whether they were placed on you intentionally or not, is three-quarters of the battle. Those tend to be the loudest and most powerful stories that we think are our own but often are not, yet have the power to shape the trajectory of what we view as our reality.

The other quarter of the effort is writing yourself into your story. It's less of the battle because your truths will surface once others' beliefs of you have been recognized and made lesser a concern in your mind. Mindset is all about taking a step back and assessing what you've accomplished and are capable of accomplishing, determining the impact you want to have, and then laying in a new trajectory for wherever direction you want your capabilities to carry you.

Don't pigeonhole yourself either. People so often will simply update their resume and conduct a job search based around their current job function. What you're doing now doesn't necessarily have to be your destiny. Challenge the status quo of your career. Give yourself permission to recognize what you're capable of doing. And for many of you, give yourself permission to question whether your loyalty to your employer, your friends, or your family is getting in the way of your loyalty to yourself.

Your Skillset: *The Best Indicator of Future Success*

Let's next review the competencies you acquired over the course of your career and, through time and effort, perfected to a high degree of mastery. This part of the process is an inventorying of the impact your talents and skills have had on each company or client you've ever worked for, or the positive effects you've had on people and various groups in your life, or how your abilities have advanced the wellness of your community.

At this point, it becomes important to distinguish talents from skills so we can understand where they intersect best to your advantage. We often use the terms talents and skills interchangeably without acknowledging how different they are from one another.

Talents are your inborn abilities or natural aptitudes. They're your proficiencies in certain activities without actually having learned or practiced them. Your actions don't require extra effort or thought on your part but seem to come naturally. Talents are not necessarily born in you either; they're often cultivated through passion, patience, and practice.

As we shared in Chapter 1, there may be talents that you have going as far back as your adolescence. You may have shelved them over the course of your life because you didn't believe them to be valuable or marketable. You may even have been convinced years ago that they wouldn't be useful talents for you to depend on as a career.

We worked with an engineer whose career inventory indicated that his number one career match was teaching. Interestingly, engineering was his worst match! From an early age, Samuel wanted to become a teacher, but his father discouraged an education degree and pressured him to instead pursue an engineering degree and become an engineer. As Samuel's father put it, *"An engineering job will allow you to better support your family. You'll make more money!"*

We learned that, as an engineer, Samuel's favorite task was mentoring and training new engineers. Through self-inquiry, his aspirations found their way to the surface and revealed to Samuel a way to bring his love of teaching into his job and ultimately transition his career to teaching full time.

Once you've thought through and cataloged your talents and skills, the next step is selecting those abilities that match the needs of the marketplace and are most tuned into your nature and purpose. We describe these as your strengths, the intersection of your talents and skills, those abilities you're truly passionate about, that come natural to you, and that you've developed over the years into personal assets. Simply put, you want to find a career that plays to your strengths.

We often use this Venn diagram in our workshops to not only bring greater attention to the intersection of your talents and skills, but to then refine that internal search and discovery with an external understanding of the needs of the marketplace.

The intersecting point where all three circles come together highlights that area where we encourage people to focus their job and career search. We call this juncture *Best Matches,* the career opportunities that will bring you the greatest sense of fulfillment; and from an employer's point of view, make you their ideal hire. Not only do those roles or careers align with your strengths, but they more closely align with your purpose in the sense that they enable you to express through your work that which comes natural to you.

Your Toolset: *Preparing and Sharing Your Story*
The third element to appraise and marshal your efforts are the resources and methods that you'll use to convey your story. Your tools could be such things as your cover letter, resume, LinkedIn profile, or website. It could

be your executive bio, a PowerPoint pitch deck, or a 30-second YouTube video. How you show up is also part of your toolset. It could be an interview suit or favorite pair of shoes that give you confidence for that face-to-face first impression.

As you go through your job or career search process, mentors and friends can also become part of your toolset. The support of those close to you can be trustworthy sounding boards for you and even open doors for you. They can help confirm and bolster your initiatives, or call you out when they think you're not being authentic.

Where Art Meets Science

Reflecting on everything we shared in this chapter, you can create all kinds of methodologies and process flows to help you move from point A, to point B, to point C over the course of your career. But at the end of the day, you have to make sure that your career ladder is on the right wall, or, as we shared in Chapter 4, that you are woven into a career lattice of your choosing, which will allow you to build the skills along your path to a career with purpose.

Putting that piece first and foremost in your career search process is what we consider the "art" component. The art is making sure that you're aiming in the right direction, that the path you're seeking and exerting your time and effort pursuing is what you really want to do in life.

As example, if you go down the path of becoming a CFO but what you really want is to own a plant nursery because horticulture is a passion of yours and you love giving people guidance, then the most fulfilling career for you would be as an owner of a plant nursery. You'd also be leveraging your financial skills.

The art is having that honest conversation with yourself that we touch on throughout this chapter. The science is in how you select and develop the tools you'll use to convey your story in the most effective way possible to ensure your resume and social media are noticed and valued by prospective employers.

Optimize Your Resume

Knowing and crafting your story is vital, but ensuring the most effective use of your resume can be equally important; it's your first most important tool. Most companies today funnel their online job application process through applicant tracking software (ATS). Be aware that these systems often cannot read text boxes, tables, color ink, or photos, or recognize any graphics. These could be eliminated from your resume and the space is left blank, meaning recruiters and hiring managers will miss those things that you're trying to stress. Submitting a resume that is easy to read is essential for it to get through these software systems.

As we shared earlier, one of the best ways to break through with a potential employer and make the most of the few seconds they'll initially give to your resume is to create a short summary statement that speaks to your talents and skills as in our "before and after" examples.

Also ensure your resume profile includes skills-specific keywords relevant to the job you are applying for and to make sure your wording of those skills is up to date and reflects current terminology. Be mindful that companies are trending away from the focus on job titles and degrees and trending more toward skills. The tracking systems we spoke of are programmed by companies to search for and prioritize the resumes that contain specific skills.

You also have to be aware of and prepare for the fact that, even in the face of all of these new technologies for tracking and cataloging applicants, the majority of our hiring clients are still very traditional in how they approach career pathing and interviewing. You need to be prepared with an optimized resume, yet one that can also pass as traditional for those recruiters and hiring managers who are still relying on old-school methods. You have to be proficient in both worlds.

Exercise: Prompts for Storytelling

To understand where you're going, you sometimes need to reflect on where you came from and the elements of your life that define who you are today. We use these 12 questions in our inquiry process to help our clients unearth the truths that become their authentic stories. The experiences in your past, if shared appropriately and creatively, can help you, as well as the world, understand who you are and what you're capable of. Use this exercise to reflect on your DNA and what comprises you before you sit down to write your story.

1. Where were you born and raised?
2. Tell me about your parents. What did they do for a living?
3. What morals and values did they instill in you regarding jobs, work, and careers? What messages were you given?
4. In what way did those morals and values serve you?
5. Tell me about your siblings.
6. What were your dreams when you were in grade school?
7. Who and what shaped you in high school? What were your dreams?
8. What happened when you left high school?
9. How did you choose your college? What significant experiences molded you?
10. Walk me through your career. Are there any roads not taken? Significant mentors? Proudest achievements?
11. What's left to do that you haven't done yet?
12. What do you want your life to look like?

6

Building Your Personal Brand

"Everyone has a chance to stand out.
Everyone has a chance to be a brand worthy of remark."
—Tom Peters

Samuel amassed an incredible resume filled with the skills and experiences he acquired over the course of his twenty-five years in business. He paid the toll though as many often do in advancing their careers. As an executive for two global companies in that span of time, Samuel traveled constantly, and when he wasn't traveling, he worked weekends. For the better part of his thirties and forties, he missed out on spending quality time with his wife, Jean, and being present in the developing lives of his two children.

When Samuel came to us, he said he was done working for large organizations and all the travel, late nights, and weekends that came with it. He wanted to work for a smaller company where he could head up operations and be home more often. You would think that a smaller organization would jump on a talent like Samuel, yet he was striking out in all of his interviews.

Each time he sat down with a recruiter or company CEO, he would speak of his accomplishments: how he managed thousands of direct and indirect employees; how he cut billions in costs across eight different manufacturing facilities in six different countries; and how he could speak three languages and negotiated deals in foreign countries.

He was missing the mark though by projecting this huge brand of himself onto these small companies with 200 employees or less. Though an impressive presentation of achievements, Samuel was talking right past them. You've heard the saying, "He didn't know his own strength." Well, Samuel didn't know the strength of his own, genuine value. He wasn't speaking to what the CEOs of these small companies wanted to hear—

how a veteran executive with global operations experience could help their business.

Unfortunately, every recruiter and leader who interviews Samuel is going to assess him as an amazing talent and a potentially huge asset, but conclude that he probably wouldn't stay for more than a few months or a year. They'll assume that the job wouldn't be challenging enough for him and that he wouldn't be content in a small-company culture. Samuel was failing to make the connection for them between his value and their need.

We coached Samuel to continue to speak of his accomplishments, but briefly and only to show his understanding of operations from different and possibly unique perspectives. We helped Samuel unearth a distinctive, more valuable brand of himself by projecting his desire to help small companies find greater efficiencies and higher profitability through the best practices he's learned and developed over the years—all scalable to a company such as theirs.

These elements of knowing your value, knowing your audience, and communicating that value in the words and ways that compel and attract are the building blocks of an authentic, persuasive personal brand.

The term "personal brand" was first introduced for public usage in Tom Peters' 1997 *Fast Company* article "The Brand Called You."[20] In it, Peters emphasizes that, regardless of age, position, the business you're in, or the type of work you do, you need to understand the importance of establishing and sustaining a personal brand. As Peters states it, *"We are CEOs of our own companies: Me Inc."*

Frankly, a lot of people think branding is nothing more than hype, but building your personal brand is really about being able to identify what you're all about. Your brand is how you talk and write about yourself, and what other people say and write about you. To that last point, Jeff Bezos, CEO of Amazon, defines your brand as *"What people say about you when you're not in the room."*

You have a reputation that is shaped by first impressions, all made lasting by the relationships your form, how you communicate, and how you collaborate. All of this impacts how others see you and remember you. If asked, your colleagues might say you're an approachable person who listens well and is easy to work with. In a sense, your personal standing in your workplace, community, and circle of friends is made up of the opinions and beliefs people form about you based on the sum of your behaviors.

While your reputation is about how credible you appear to others, your personal brand is how *you want* people to see you and the personal values, capabilities, and beliefs that you want others to know about you. What the facets of yourself are that set you distinctly apart—much like a fingerprint—from anyone else.

Gaining Momentum

The practice of building a personal brand has rapidly grown over the past several years. We believe that drive has been fueled by the younger generations' quest for purpose and meaning in their careers. From that perspective, personal brand becomes the outward expression of their character, their mission, what they want to accomplish, and what they want their legacy to be.

What has added oxygen and accelerated that momentum is the growth of social media and the forming of *digital brands*, the virtual representation of who we are as individuals. Our digital brand consists of so many artifacts now including resumes, social media profiles, personal websites, apps, YouTube videos, even email signatures. It includes anything you've ever written and published on LinkedIn, Facebook, Twitter, TikTok, or other platforms. It includes your past speaking engagements, podcasts, professional activities at work, and volunteerism in your personal life.

With the building of your personal brand in mind, Chapter 6 actually becomes an extension of Chapter 5, for once you know your story and can speak to it, building your personal brand around that story completes your outward expression and presentation of yourself. This chapter is designed to help you refine your story as we work through together the **Four Steps to Building Your Personal Brand**: 1) know your value, the relationship of your story to your brand; 2) know your audience, their needs, content expectations, and preferred sources and formats of information; 3) communicate to your audience by translating your brand into words and images; and 4) build a network of supporters who sustain you by inspiring, trusting, and following you.

Four Steps to Building Your Personal Brand

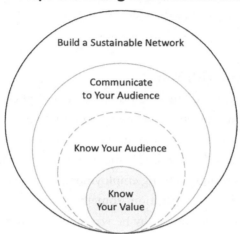

Build a Sustainable Network

Communicate
to Your Audience

Know Your Audience

Know
Your Value

Each step provides the illustrations, strategies, exercises, and resources that will help you home in on what you value most; make the connection of that value to your audience; and communicate it with consistency and confidence. The first, inner-most circle is being in touch with who and what you are at the core of your being.

1) Know Your Value

The first step in any sound construction project is laying the right foundation. In the context of brand building, knowing your value is that foundation. While Chapter 5 focused on unearthing your story, knowing your value is the relationship of your story to your value and is two-fold: understanding your story and personal value; and communicating that value to your audience. In a sense, this first step is determining what your "why" is, what you're all about deep within you. "Why" is the acknowledgment of what's important to you, what you're going to stand for, and what will receive your full commitment.

Simon Sinek, David Mead, and Peter Docker talk about the importance of knowing yourself and what you stand for in their book, *Find Your Why: A Practical Guide for Discovering Purpose for You and Your Team.* [21] Their essential point is that we are all entitled to wake up in the morning feeling inspired to go to work, feeling safe when we're there, and returning home fulfilled at the end of the day. Achieving that fulfillment starts with understanding exactly why we do what we do.

Coming to Terms with Your Value

Antonio is a 62-year-old business professional and phenomenal salesperson. He walked into his office one morning only to find that he no longer had a job. He was angry and quite upset when he came to us after having spent two months with the outplacement services his company provided and having no traction in finding employment. He was singularly focused on landing a similar sales position, something he could speak to all day long, but couldn't understand why he was striking out finding new work. Now, ageism is a very real thing and an increasing problem in recruitment, but that's not always the roadblock.

By our second session, we were able to reveal to Antonio how he came across in our mock interviews when telling his story: angry, cynical, frustrated, and anxious. Antonio was giving the impression of being quite spiteful and potentially difficult to work with. And no one wants to hire an angry person, regardless of their skills and experience.

We helped Antonio shift his attention to building a new foundation by coming to terms with his core value and intersecting that new perception of himself with what he truly wanted to do next in his career. Knowing his own story and being able to tell it has brought Antonio new content, a deeper presence during interviews, and renewed traction. A genuine, personal brand has emerged in Antonio and he's now able to tell his story in a much different way and with greater confidence and ease.

Antonio came to a deeper understanding of what it was that gave him joy in his work. He realized that it didn't have to be a lifetime of being on the front lines; his joy could be helping others to become successful salespeople by sharing what he had learned over the past 25 years. This became quite a shift in purpose for Antonio. He no longer aims to be the sales executive he once was. He now views his past as a building block that has enabled him to become a sales coach and mentor to the younger generations.

When first meeting and speaking with individuals about their careers, we often find them so caught up in trying to fill an existing position. We see it in how they go about writing their resumes, promoting themselves, and responding to our mock interview questions. Once we get to know them, we find the vast majority have created personas of themselves that really don't represent their true intentions and interests. That suppression of their value and real aspirations actually makes it harder for recruiters, interviewers, coaches, mentors, or sponsors to guide them toward a career that's the best fit for them.

Many people mold themselves into a role and soon realize it's not the job or career that really suits them and has them hopping out of bed in the morning. The average time now in a role for a millennial or Generation Z is a little over two years. Quite a drop from past generations. Young people early in their careers are jumping ship all the time in their quest to shoehorn themselves into something instead of admitting, *"This is who I am and what you'll get from me that's genuine."*

That transparency is precisely what companies are looking for today and seldom finding. You have to know how to talk about your value in the context of the opportunity presented to you. Learn what the company is all about and why you connect to them. Be willing to talk about that connection and draw yourself into their story. You'll be more memorable and appealing because people are looking for that kind of presence and genuineness. No one values the corporate suit who's there simply to fill a role.

Jennifer applied for a director of engineering position for a very large manufacturing firm in the Midwest. Her resume brimmed with impressive accomplishments and the leadership team was anxious to meet her. This was a key position they were trying to fill and they anticipated huge potential in her. While her resume got her in the door, she still had to navigate the interview process. This was Jennifer's opportunity to leave a lasting impression. Unfortunately, she spent the majority of her time talking about her accomplishments and responding to questions with uninspiring answers. At the end of the day, she failed to get the job.

The company was looking for someone who could lead a global team and create a more collaborative culture. They needed a director who was skilled and experienced at aligning the efforts of individual team members toward a shared goal. They didn't hear any of that coming out of Jennifer. Instead, she responded with words and a persona she thought they would want to hear and see. She may have been the best person for the job, but she didn't create an emotional, genuine connection with them. No one cares that you've worked at a Fortune 100 company or worked internationally, or have a PhD if they don't see a connection to why your brand is important to their business.

What Makes You Different?

A critical component of knowing your brand's value is getting to the nub of what makes your product (you) different. Ask yourself the same question brand managers at Ford, Coke, or L'Oréal ask themselves: *"What is it that my product or service does that makes it different and better?"*

Let's try an exercise. Just as the brand manager of the Ford F150 would define the characteristics of their pickup truck that distinguish it from a Chevy Silverado, start by identifying the qualities or characteristics that make you distinctive from others in your career of interest. What would your friends, co-workers, customers, or clients say is your greatest, most apparent strength? What would they say is the best personal trait about you?

Now, what are the assets that you want to be known for? Assets are a reflection of who you are and what you do. They're what you build your brand around. They could be the hard and soft _skills_ you've gained through experience. Your assets could be your _passions_, those things that you invest time and resources to ameliorate. They could be your _credentials_ or licenses that demonstrate your expertise. Finally, your assets could be your core _values and beliefs_.

Employers want to hire people who share similar ideals. In the space below, name the asset(s) that you want to be known for by your audience. Imagine you're speaking with someone at a networking event and you want to convey your value in a sentence.

> *The asset(s) that I want to be known for...*
>
>
>
>
>
>
>
>
>

2) Know Your Audience

Once you have an idea of what to say, knowing your audience's most pressing needs, the content they're looking for, and their preferred sources and formats of information can guide you toward the appropriate substance, tone, vehicle, and voice of your communications.

As example, just as it was with the advent of Facebook, LinkedIn, and Twitter, TikTok is the latest app to explode onto social media. LAK Group is right there using it to communicate to specific audiences. We'll show you an example later in this chapter. Our consumers are expanding in their information consumption preferences and patterns and we want to be right along there with them.

We are very intentional about communicating to a younger professional. We want to make sure that we're seen as adaptive and creative with some of the new technology and not fixed in our own ways. We realize that we can't be relevant employing the same traditional way that we used to build our business at the start and TikTok will now help to strengthen our brand.

In the space provided, identify an audience that you intend to communicate to and list their specific need(s). What matter of content are they looking for that would address those needs? Additionally, what channels of information are most relevant and preferred by this group?

My audience:

The need(s) that I can uniquely serve and the content they're seeking:

Their preferred sources and formats for information:

---

3) Communicate to Your Audience

Knowing your value and your audience's needs are two critical steps in building your personal brand. However, these two elements comprise less than half the equation. The greater task is in communicating your value.

How your brand translates into the written word is where the rubber really grips the road. Earlier, we shared at length the evolution of the resume, the first document people typically create to summarize their responsibilities and accomplishments and highlight their skills. We shared how to build a resume beginning with the *summary statement*—the culmination and refinement of your entire story into one short paragraph with evidence of your story's authenticity. With building your brand in mind, let's review your resume again, particularly your summary paragraph.

When communicating to your audience, specifically through a resume, your brand must emerge at the onset. Your summary statement should be the first entry point in written word of your brand in its entirety. That will then be translated into the "about" section of your LinkedIn profile, then Facebook, Twitter, Tumblr, Reddit, Instagram, TikTok, or any platform that you leverage on a regular basis.

Your goal is consistency in messaging across all of those mediums. Social media is no place to appear duplicitous or conflicted in your identity and beliefs. Now, the exact wording you would use on your LinkedIn sections may not be the same as on your Facebook postings or Twitter tweets or TikTok videos. They all must be related yet tailored to what that audience expects to read or see in that particular medium.

Your personal brand even extends to your email signature and your name as it appears with or without your middle name or initial, your title, and how best to reach you. Even the epigraph following your signature is part of your brand. It's really an outward expression of your beliefs.

Have an intention for your timing and frequency in releasing your content by keeping your audience's preferences in mind, whether it's Tuesdays at the start of day or Thursdays after lunch. Also ensure that you're focusing on different delivery methods such as podcasts, HTML email, video conferences, speaking engagements, blogs, and articles.

Create Messages that Break Through

Our senses are flooded with hundreds of messages each day and, as a matter of survival (and sanity) we've become very selective about what we'll let into our protected field of attention. Organizations go as far as developing software programs to screen messages, treating their attention as a scarce resource. To stay on top, your message must be unique, clear, and impactful. *Forbes'* four steps to crafting a strong brand message serves as a useful model for creating messages that break through.[22]

Identify your objective. What do you want your audience to do when they focus on your message? Do you want them to reply to your email, give you a call, sign up for something, accept your invite for a Zoom presentation, or purchase what you're offering? The action you want your audience to take has to be clearly spelled out.

Pick your messaging style. Establish a tone for your message that reflects your brand and echoes your target audience's style and preferences. When picking your style, focus on the audience's perspective and the tone and formats that contour to your product or service offering. Step into your audience's shoes and try to understand what they're looking for and how and when they want to receive information.

Tell a story. Our brains tend to recall stories better than plain facts. Organizational psychologist Peg Neuhauser found that learning which flows from a well-told story is remembered more thoroughly, and for far longer, than learning sourced from statistics. Research suggests that facts are 20 times more likely to be remembered if they're part of a story.[23]

Deliver it. Your audience will consist of various kinds of people who absorb information differently. Therefore, you should strive to share your message in relevant formats (audio, video, blog, articles, etc.) and on multiple appropriate channels (web and social media).

Let's apply this model to your message for a reality check on how each step reflects your personal brand.

What immediate action do you want your audience to take?

What are your audience's communication style preferences?

What are three stories that you can develop and use to support your facts?

Where does your audience source their information relevant to your brand?

Create Your Digital Brand

Let's use Mike Milsted as an example to show you the consistency that he has built up in his digital brand, from his LinkedIn "about" section, to his website, to his TikTok career tip videos. Digital brand is much more than just words; it's also images. For instance, you never would have known that Mike was a motorcycle rider until you've seen him riding around his hometown or on the Tail of the Dragon in North Carolina, or visited his website. The Tail of the Dragon is considered one of the world's best motorcycling and sports car roads. It's both an exciting and beautiful 11-mile stretch of highway with its 318 curves, winding along the southwest boundary of the Great Smoky Mountains National Park.

If you Google "Mike Milsted," what appears first at the top of the search results is his LAK Group bio. You'll find that the first sentence in his profile, right up front, speaks to his passion:

As a president and partner with the LAK Group, Mike Milsted has a strong desire to help people find meaningful involvement in what they do because aligning people and business is his passion.

The next search result flags Mike's LinkedIn profile. In his "about" section, he expounds on his passion and purpose, but also shares more about what drives him and makes him human. Here's how it reads:

I strive to live my values, to create balance in my life and to have a meaningful impact on others. On Purpose.

I am driven by a passion to engage people and organizations in their purpose and to find meaningful involvement in all they do. At LAK Group, we empower the mission of inspiring people to identify the impact they desire to have and inspire them to have the courage to live their passion with purpose.

I am made of an old dusty farmhouse in the country, family advocacy, and the resilience and grit I learned from my parents. I consider myself to be a 'Dadrepreneur,' and I seek to understand the needs of organizations, business leaders, and human resources to solve issues surrounding strategy, talent management, leadership coaching, mentoring, change management, succession planning, retention, and assessment (to name a few).

I seek to understand the needs of organizations and business leaders to solve issues surrounding strategy, talent management, leadership coaching, mentoring, change management, succession planning, retention, and assessment. I serve as a sounding board for my clients to solve complex issues with simple solutions. I am an advisor in the management consulting industry helping employers address the changing demands of digital transformation. I've helped my customers balance the ideals of leadership development and career development, management, and planning to enable people and their personal brand.

I started as a Social Worker at an area family advocacy shelter and currently volunteer with the Boy Scouts of America, National Kidney Foundation and Habitat for Humanity. I have embraced a career dedicated to having a meaningful impact on people's lives. I've been fortunate to work with companies of all shapes and sizes from Fortune 100 global firms to small and medium businesses on main street.

When people network with Mike, he can tell if they've read his LinkedIn profile the second they ask him, *"Mike, what's a dadpreneur?"* Mike loves starting conversations around that concept. That word is put there deliberately to draw people in, as is the image of Mike on his motorcycle, his involvement with Habitat for Humanity, or being a Boy Scout leader. He can't count the number of times those mentions have attracted people to him and made them immediately comfortable speaking with him.

The next search result is Mike's website, www.mikemilsted.com. Here you can learn about Mike and his personal involvements and passions in greater depth, check out his videos and blogs, and learn how to reach Mike. You'll find in all of his mediums a consistency in his digital brand. It's right there on his home page.

I strive to live my values, to create balance in my life and to have a meaningful impact on others. On Purpose.

Driven by a passion to engage people and organizations in their purpose and to find meaningful involvement in what they do, I joined LAK Group to empower my mission: to embolden people to identify the impact they desire to have in life, and to inspire them to have the courage to live their passion...

Mike's words and images are his color commentary that adds a flavor to who he is, and yours should build and extend the same way for you as well. Your intent is to use multiple avenues to tell your story and, in a variety of ways, speak to who you are. Building a personal brand is not just being able to define what you're all about, but to do so in a self-expressive way that's genuine and draws people of like minds and interests toward you.

Our intent at LAK Group is to use these platforms for specific purposes while maintaining consistent themes. We've decided to have a brand presence on TikTok with focus on career advice for individuals and organizations. This link will take you to our online page on TikTok: www.tiktok.com/@lakgroup. You'll immediately see over a dozen thumbnails of video clips of varying lengths from 15 seconds to three minutes of Mike Milsted delivering a **Pro Career Tip of the Day**. Here's an example of one.

Hey there folks, Mike here with your pro career tip of the day. We're going to talk a bit about how to answer that question that pretty much always comes up in interviews: "Tell me about yourself." Or when you're introducing yourself to someone. You don't want to go into this without having a strategy and without practicing. Think through the strategy of a past, present, and future characterization of yourself.

What did you do in the past that's relevant to your audience? What do you do currently? And what do you hope to be able to do?

If you think through that strategy and practice, practice, practice, you're going to put together a really compelling argument about who you are and who you're going to be. It really helps people get a good sense for what you're all about. And remember, you have to practice.

We hope our TikTok messaging will become a valuable career advice hack with thought-provoking ideas and tips for people seeking a career with purpose. You'll find advice on questions to ask yourself if you're thinking about leaving your organization, or how to conduct your daily job search, or how to best manage your time. You'll find supportive ideas on how to speak about your value and I'll give you questions you can ask during interviews to ensure that company is the best fit for you.

Mike's TikTok platform may push a different narrative than that found on his LinkedIn profile or personal website, yet all three are telling different parts of the same story. The idea in digital branding is to understand the realm of possibilities and then to communicate in meaningful ways on each of those platforms tuned to audience expectations and preferences.

Your brand should not be repelling, confrontational, or defensive. It should attract people toward you and your story. It should genuinely reflect how you *want* your audience to see you and the personal values, capabilities, and beliefs that encompass your brand.

Recruiters and company personnel can distinguish real and substantive content from hollow pretentiousness in a heartbeat. They can also tell a lot about a person by their passions and hobbies, their volunteerism, the organizations they belong to, and other digital brands they associate with. You have it within you to shape how you are seen by the world. Be genuine and consistent in communicating your value.

4) Build a Network that Sustains You

The last step in building your personal brand is to create a network of people who will sustain your presence and value. This is about creating followership, your ability to inspire, to build relationships and to build your credibility with others so that people will trust and follow you.

There's a great deal of networking today that takes place outside of corporate America. Advances in video conferencing have made networking easier and far reaching when you consider the ability to connect with your audience across the country or around the world. Creating a network of followers who will think of your brand when an opportunity arises is your ultimate goal. You want people to think of you first and to think of you often.

Building a network that follows and supports you can be accomplished a number of different ways. The followers that you have on LinkedIn are a valuable start. You can also create special interest groups or host "meet-ups" in your city or community that encourage your followers to be more active and engaged.

As example, www.meetup.com is a social networking resource that allows you to find and join groups related to your own personal interests. People use Meetup to meet new people, learn new things, find support, get out of their comfort zones, and pursue their passions. However, instead of just talking about these interests online, Meetup is used to either join or organize offline and in-person meetings in your area. Live meetups or events are often the best way to create true engagement with your community as they allow you to have clear face-to-face time and make real connections over the things that matter.

The tips and techniques you learned in this chapter on knowing your value, knowing your audience, and communicating that value in the words and ways that compel and attract will help you bring to life your authentic, persuasive personal brand. Moreover, these insights, along with your preparation, will help you build the confidence and presence you'll need to succeed in the next most important step in your career journey—the job interview.

Questions to Reflect On

1. What is your value and how does it relate to your story, the substance of who you are?

2. What are three ways people would describe you?

3. How do you *want* people to see you? What are the personal values, capabilities, and beliefs that you want others to know about you?

4. With your most important audience in mind, what needs of theirs can you uniquely serve?

5. How do you communicate your value? What words and images do you use to convey that value? Are you consistent in communicating your value in social media?

6. What efforts are you taking to create a network of people who will sustain your presence and value and build your credibility with others?

7

How to Show Up in the Interview

*"One important key to success is self-confidence.
An important key to self-confidence is preparation."*
—Arthur Ashe

Building and communicating your personal brand are critical steps in finding a career with purpose. The digital brand presence that you create becomes the outward expression of your character, what you aspire to do in your work life and for whom, and what you want your legacy to be.

Interviewing, the focus of this chapter, and *networking*, the emphasis of Chapter 8, are the two key undertakings that will carry you beyond your digital presence and help distinctly communicate your brand to others. Both endeavors require you being actively involved and out there voicing who you are and exemplifying what you can uniquely bring to an organization.

Your performance in these two activities, particularly in the first weeks of your job search, will translate into success or failure in finding a job and career that truly speaks to your interests. We find that beginning this process correctly can truly make a difference in your outcome.

An interviewing competency is something we develop first in our clients to address the more pressing need in those earliest weeks where performance truly counts. By interviewing competency, we mean being aware of the organization's interview strategy and having one of your own. It's knowing their approach for determining if you fit the skills requirements of the position and align with the cultural behaviors and values of the organization. However, the most important aspect of your interviewing competency is knowing what *your* strategy is for communicating your talents and skills and expressing your cultural fit and passion for the job.

The Mistakes People Make

Over the course of your career, you've no doubt become familiar with the classic truisms for "interviewing success"—dress for success, arrive on time, research the employer, and follow up with a thank you letter or email. But there are other things to take into consideration that can not only determine your success in interviewing, but also your success in finding a career with meaning and lasting value.

Without question, nerves play a big part in the interview process and everyone has areas that they could improve upon. However, more often than not, it's the most preventable errors that can cost you the job or cause you to accept a position that falls short of your expectations. Through our practice we have identified the Top Seven Mistakes people typically make while interviewing; mistakes that with proper foresight in planning and mental preparation can be controlled for and make all the difference in your outcome.

1) Placing Content Over Culture

What we consider the greatest mistake people can make in their preparation and during the interviewing process is not one that you'll commonly hear about or read on career sites and blogs. People in "job search mode" will often make the mistake of walking into an interview singularly focused on the tangibles such as title, salary, and benefits. They're so absorbed in whether the position is going to be a good step for them in their career that they'll overlook researching the culture of the organization. Many young people commit this error by rationalizing to themselves, *"I won't be there for more than a couple of years. I'll leverage my new title and higher salary in my next move."*

It's not uncommon for a person to land the dream title and find that the company and job fail to provide them the opportunity to gain real experience at this point in their career. They may find that the company has little to no vision or doesn't share their values; that there are no learning and development programs for employees; or that leadership is slow to adopting innovation and change. From a personal standpoint, they may discover that the position has no autonomy in decision making or budget authorization, or no direct reporting line to the senior leader or CEO.

Focusing on content only without sufficient thought or concern for the culture of the company can limit your marketability later on in your career. You may walk into a future interview with a big title and salary, but potential employers will pass on you if you lack the experience and wisdom.

How do you really get to know a company's culture without having worked there? Websites such as Glassdoor, Indeed, and LinkedIn can shed some light through the reviews posted by the prospective company's employees. Clearly, the best way to know the culture of an organization is by talking with the people who currently work there or have recently left for opportunities elsewhere. They'll provide valuable insights into the company's leadership effectiveness, management style, working environment, values, and more.

2) Over-Preparing

The second most detrimental mistake people make is managing their nervous energy by poring over material and memorizing financials and facts about the company and its industry right up to the night before the interview. They'll dig deep into each competitor and review what employees on Glassdoor or Indeed are saying about their leadership team, management style, and opportunities available to employees.

They amass so much data to the point where all those facts and figures get in the way of them being themselves, and it causes many to lose their composure. The more they try to commit to memory, the more they forget about their own story and the questions they planned on asking their interviewers.

Clients who are successful in their job search often tell us that they attribute their doing well to the take-it-or-leave-it approach they conveyed during their interview as opposed to appearing anxious and needful. Although they truly cared about the role being presented, their calm demeanor and thoughtful questions conveyed a self-confident, pleasant attitude that set their interviewers at ease as well.

The best way to negotiate anything to your favor is to be willing to walk away from the deal. Ask the questions that you need to ask and continue asking them until you get the answers you're looking for. Your objective is not to state your demands, but to determine if the culture of the company suits you and the position gives you the experience and growth you're seeking. A take-it-or-leave-it attitude is powerful because it signifies that you're someone who has personal standards and values that are non-negotiable— the very kind of principled, thoughtful person companies are looking to hire.

3) Not Having Questions

Not preparing questions in advance to ask of the interviewers is in essence suggesting to recruiters, HR representatives, and hiring managers that you have no strong convictions or personal expectations of your own. It may also indicate to them that you may not really be interested in their company, department, or team. These are not the best impressions to leave of yourself. In our mock interviews, people will often say at the end of our session, *"I don't think I have any more questions."* There has to be something!

We suggest that you continue to ask questions until the interviewer says the session is over. This means that you have to be prepared with questions to ask of every interviewer. One approach is to ask the same question of different interviewers to see if there's consistency in their responses. Ask an intangible question on culture to confirm that the environment you're looking for truly exists. As example, you could ask each interviewer, *"What meaning and sense of satisfaction does working here give you?"*

4) Not Preparing at All

Over-preparing is a big mistake, but not gathering any information on an organization, the role that you're interviewing for, and the people you're speaking with is a huge blunder as well. You are not prepared if you know nothing about the company or its industry, what type of work it does or the services it provides, its culture and values, and most especially, details of the position you've applied for.

It will be painfully obvious to your interviewer if you didn't do your research ahead of time, especially when you don't have questions stemming from your research, or you can only give generic, dispassionate answers to questions such as, *"Why do you want to work here?"* or *"What do you know about our culture?"* You may be the very best at what you do and a potentially valuable addition to a company that hires you, but not preparing at all is not what companies expect of their employees.

5) Preparing Improperly

This mistake is an unfortunate by-product of over-preparing. Learning how to manage your own nervous energy is one thing, but you can take it too far. For instance, what are you doing the night before your interview? Are you stressed out reviewing as much information as possible on the company, or are you relaxing and enjoying your evening with your family, having dinner with your significant other or a friend, or watching a comedy on television?

It's a lot like stressing the night before final exams and coming to the realization, as you stare in shock at your grade, that what you didn't know the night before the test, you didn't know during the test. Doing your homework on the organization is important, but this mistake is more about undervaluing the soft side of preparation—believing in the good job you did in preparing and feeling self-assured and composed the night before.

6) Reciting Your Skills and Capabilities

It may be a sign of nervousness or due to a lack of preparation, but a mistake people often make is responding to the question, *"Tell me about your role at Acme Company,"* by reciting their resume that's sitting right in front of them and the interviewer and unexcitingly saying, *"I led a team."*

Bring your resume to life through storytelling. Tell the hiring manager what you accomplished with that team, how you created an esprit de corps among team members who represented different departments in the organization and how you were the glue that held them together. Tell the story of how you were able to manage their efforts and keep them aligned, informed, and highly productive even though they didn't report to you; and tell them how you were able to keep the project on time and under budget. You have one opportunity to tell your story and captivate the hiring manager. Don't get overly complicated and always relate your experience back to the company you're interviewing with and what their challenges and goals are.

7) Expecting to Be Interviewed

A huge mistake people make is going into the interview expecting be interviewed. Having that attitude will never work in your favor. You are the initiator of this entire process and have to show up with that attitude. You need to know if the company is going to be a good fit for you, not just let them learn if you're a good fit for the company.

The interview process is for both you and the prospective employer to size each other up to ensure compatibility and future happiness. With that mindset, have it become the guiding force in your research and preparation of questions. You can be certain that the company will be investing their time as well as scrutinizing your background, personality traits, and cultural fit to see if you're the one. Besides, most all organizations like interviewees who ask a lot of questions; it's an indication to them that you're going to be an engaged, involved employee.

There's another aspect of the mistake of expecting to be interviewed that really isn't a mistake. You *should* expect to be interviewed, but you should expect to be interviewed well! One of the biggest errors hiring managers make is showing up to the interview completely unprepared. Do you really want to work for a person who hasn't taken the time to learn about you and your background? This could be an indication of what it may be like to work for this person—that they will seldom have time for you or know the value of your contribution. A job interview is a two-way street where both parties need to be committed to discovering each other to ensure a perfect fit.

Interviewing with Purpose

Avoiding mistakes is one thing, but you can't win on defense alone. To find a career with purpose, you need to interview with purpose, which means viewing yourself as the instigator and driver of the interview process. Your goal is to determine if the job and the organization align with your purpose in work and in life. You don't want to accept a position, then three months later realize that the job and company were not what you expected.

Recall our story in Chapter 4 about Brian, who was told by his new manager (as she showed him the door) that he wasn't leadership material and that he should focus his efforts on looking for another analyst position. His manager misguided Brian in his job search and put him on the wrong career path. Not only did his resume reflect it, but it showed in how he interviewed as well and how he recoiled from what was offered him—a position two levels higher than what he interviewed for.

When Brian received the offer letter, he shared his concern with us because he didn't know if he should accept the role, given what his former manager had drummed into him about his limitations. We coached Brian on how to respond to the offer and ask the kinds of questions that could help determine if the role was really suited for him. Brian got the answers that he wanted and ended up getting re-offered at a higher salary because of his line of inquiry, which indicated to the hiring company that he was more than capable of handling the responsibility of the position. The job being offered was two levels above where he had been in the company that just laid him off. Yet, it was at the level that he needed to be at and was clearly capable of stepping into.

Brian was "interviewing down" out of an anxiousness to find work and still believing what his manager had told him he should settle for. The process of self-realization was a critical turning point in Brian's career search. We clearly recognized that he had the capabilities; it was a matter of him finding that out for himself.

Interviewing with purpose is identifying those things that are important to your career and will bring motivation and purpose to your life. These are your personal and professional satisfiers that you must have fulfilled when you're searching for the right job or career. To that end, there are **Three Steps to Interviewing with Purpose** that will put you in control and ensure a mutually beneficial outcome for you and your prospective employer: (1) having an interview strategy; (2) being present in the interview; and (3) planning your follow-up.

Step 1: Have an Interview Strategy

You have most likely heard this saying more than once in your life, *"You only get one chance to make a first impression."* Research supports this age-old maxim and points to the power and effect of those first few moments in an interview.

- First impressions are formed, on average, within 12 seconds.[24]

- Hiring managers admit that 33 percent of hiring decisions are made within 90 seconds of meeting someone. To put that into perspective, it takes the average person 90 seconds to write a response to a text message.[25] If you had 90 seconds, what impression would you want to leave?

- In face-to-face meetings, 93 percent of the interviewer's assessment of you will be based on what you didn't say, sourcing from nonverbal input such as your facial expressions, eye contact, tone of voice, body movement and posture, and attire.[26]

If you walk into an interview and commit the mistakes that we listed above and don't show active interest and involvement, then you're bound to make a very poor first impression. We coach people in the process of outplacement to "go slow to go fast." Take a deep breath. You may have been thrust into the job search market, as Brian was in the story above, and are feeling the pressure to find a new job as quickly as possible. Nevertheless, the most important advice we can give you is to get organized first and develop your interview strategy. We have found time and again that the preparations that you make in the first two weeks of your search will have a profound impact on the duration of time you're unemployed.

For starters, your strategy is to know the role that you're interviewing for, the company you're interviewing with, its industry, and the trends in that industry. For example, if you're interviewing with Baxter Pharmaceutical Company, it's best to know how Boston Scientific, Abbott, Medtronic, and others are responding to breakthroughs in precision medicine, bioprinting technologies, or new regulations in the pharmaceutical industry.

If you're interviewing in the financial or insurance fields, you could initiate a discussion by saying, *"Tell me a little bit about the combined versus uncombined ratio underwriting costs."* In other words, *"How profitable is your company at writing business as an insurer?"* Knowing what's trending in the prospective employer's industry is a great source for questions to ask.

Dun & Bradstreet (www.dnb.com) is one of the top credit reporting agencies and is another valuable resource that provides business intelligence products to clients through its database and analytics software.

You can review a company's 10K and 10Q, the CEO's letter to the shareholders, their annual reports that outline the strategies your prospective employer implemented the prior year, and their successes or failures. Look for their plans for the current year and over the course of the next five years. This is a great source for your questions, which will show the depth of your interest in them.

Another valuable resource for conducting research on industries and companies and questions you could ask of your interviewers is https://www.onetonline.org. There are also very active chambers of commerce that work closely with private employers in their cities. They will often be the first to have information on companies moving in or out or expanding their operations before they officially broadcast their intentions to the business media.

All of the above are just some of the examples of the online resources available to you in developing an interviewing strategy. However, the best source of information often underestimated and overlooked is your network, a subject we'll cover in depth in Chapter 8. As it relates to knowing about the company you're interviewing with, a well-developed network can advance your knowledge with valuable information that you may not find in generally available research.

Knowing What Matters Most to You

Aside from knowing the company and the industry, a critical dimension of your interview strategy is knowing yourself and knowing what's important to you. If culture is critical and you're contemplating leaving your present situation or you've already left because of your manager, which is really a symptom of the culture of that organization, know how to ask questions that will specifically uncover what matters most to you. For example, *"What does working here allow you to do that has meaning in your personal life?"*

Ask that question of every person you interview, for it's the consistency of that theme across the organization that you're seeking, right up through to the CEO. How would you ask the CEO that question? Consider asking them, *"How does this organization impact the lives of the customers that use its products and why is that important to you?"*

It's interesting how people answer the question of meaning in their work lives. Sometimes it's the lack of an answer that can be quite revealing. That moment of silence can speak volumes if the interviewer hasn't thought about it or there's no deeper meaning beyond it being a job to them. Keep in mind that it's not that way everywhere though. Ask any employee at Google that question and they'll most likely say, *"I want to be Googling,"* meaning they want to be creative and being a Google employee inspires and enables that in them. When you interview with Google, you're being interviewed not just for what you know, but who you are.

We often conduct mock interviews as live learning events dedicated to (1) the questions that you will most likely get asked; and (2) the questions that you should be prepared to ask. In the appendix at the end of this chapter, you'll find the Top Ten Questions that interviewees are typically asked and tips on how best to respond to each. In the appendix, you'll also find Questions You Should Ask of recruiters, HR representatives, and hiring managers to ensure that you are interviewing with purpose and that the company and job are a meaningful and satisfying fit for you.

Step 2: Be Present in the Interview

Having presence in the interview is being mindfully in attendance, meaning you're focused, engaged, and thoughtful of your role and responsibilities. The more present you are, the better chance you have of having a genuine dialogue with someone rather than just showing up to be questioned!

Being present is being able to drown out all the other distractions in your world and instead concentrating on that person and leaning into your conversation with them with enthusiasm. We often associate presence with curiosity. Being curious is listening to understand and not just to respond to questions. When you're curious, you're thinking of broader contexts and actively trying to apply what you're learning about the position and the company to what's important to you.

Another component of presence is your body language. We have so many experiences of people in our mock interviews who slouch in their chairs and fail to maintain eye contact. They're unaware of how their body language communicates disengagement and lack of interest.

Interview eye contact is critical. If you're not engaging with your eyes, people are not going to connect with you. It's a real turnoff when you don't look someone in the eye when you're answering or asking questions and a real turn-on when you do.

Your articulation, enunciation, and tone of voice convey presence as well. One of the things we teach in our Executive Presence sessions is to make sure that your communication is clear and concise. Articulation is the ability to use a broad range of words with effect while enunciation is how clearly you speak those words. Many interviewees mumble out of uncertainty or talk too fast out of nervousness. Know what you want to say and be measured and intentional in your delivery.

In addition to having an interview strategy for physical face-to-face, one-on-one interviews, you should be prepared for and have a strategy in place if the interview is online, if there's more than one interviewer in the room, or if you've been asked to submit a video of yourself answering the prospective employer's questions—what we term AI Interviewing.

Video-Conferenced Interviews

The virtual interview is an adaptation that you should be ready for as part of your digital brand presence. First and foremost, find a suitable backdrop for your interview. One approach is to use a plain, uncluttered wall behind you. If appropriate to the position you're seeking, you can also use your background to express personality and convey certain aspects of your personal brand.

Ensure your camera is positioned so you're making direct eye contact with the person or people on the other end of the call. Level your camera so it appears you're positioned across from the interviewer at eye level. If you're using a laptop screen, prop up your laptop so you're not looking down on the interviewer. Whether intentional or not, looking down on someone is a nonverbal communication of power and can be very unsettling for the person on the receiving end. In virtual interviews, proper lighting is also important as is what you're wearing, but eye contact is the most critical factor. Eye contact in a virtual setting is analogous to a firm handshake when you're face-to-face with someone. Both convey confidence, self-worth, and interest in the other person.

Panel Interviews

In some instances, you'll find companies trying to bring in as many candidates as possible to interview for a position and will sometimes conduct panel interviews involving two or more interviewers at once. It's not uncommon to have as many as 12 or more—a whole jury of interviewers! Their intent is to speed up the hiring process by having one set of questions posed to each interviewee and each panelist assigned a specific question from that set. In this fashion, the entire panel can hear the interviewee's response at the same time.

Understand that there will be a number of different personalities all looking for responses that address their specific needs or expectations. You want to be careful not to cater your response solely to the person who is asking the question. Each person on the panel represents the company so your response should be to everyone.

Don't be distracted, intimidated, or discouraged by interviewers checking their phones, fidgeting, or stepping out to take an important call.

These may be high-level leaders and managers who were called in at the last minute and may not have a complete perspective of you as a candidate. Nevertheless, they'll get a chance to meet you, ask questions, and rely on their first impressions of you. Be mentally prepared for those disruptions to the interviewing schedule. Use it as an opportunity to show your flexibility, adaptability, and calm in the face of chaos.

Additionally, there's going to be a lot of dead air in a panel interview while the interviewers coordinate with each other who's going to ask what next and generally talk amongst themselves. This may present an opportunity for you to keep the dialogue going by asking a question yourself. You'll be showing your intent to participate in the discussion evenly, as an equal partner in their learning about you and you learning about them.

AI Interviews

More and more companies today are using artificial intelligence (AI) programs to conduct automated video interviews of candidates who record themselves on an interview platform and answer questions under time pressure. Their videos are then submitted through an AI platform, which processes the candidate's visual (smiles, frowns), verbal (key words used), and vocal (tone of voice) responses. The program then sends a report with an interpretation of the job candidate's performance to the employer.[27]

Many young people are already familiar and confident in this medium given that the technology is similar to recording a TikTok or YouTube video. However, the difference in this instance is that you typically will not have questions in advance. The tips we shared above in Video-Conferenced Interviews apply to this format as well.

In addition, prepare for an AI interview by making practice recordings of you answering likely questions to ensure that you're concise and not rambling. Also check that you're articulating and enunciating your words properly. Make sure that you maintain eye contact while you respond and that your facial expressions, physical movements, and hand gestures convey a calm, quiet confidence.

Preparing for interviews reminds us of a funny story: A gentleman goes to New York to attend a concert, but gets lost. He sees a woman carrying a violin case and asks, *"Ma'am, can you tell me how to get to Carnegie Hall?"* The musician smiles and says, *"Practice, practice, practice."*

Having an interview strategy enables you to take control and show them who you are. If you don't tell your story your way—with a mindfulness to not dominate the interview but to create dialogue—they're going to define your story for you. Be present in the interview by knowing what your strengths and passions are and the proof points that demonstrate those themes, and by being ready to have that conversation.

Step 3: Plan Your Follow-Up

People often ask what the best strategies are for following up after the interview. Do you craft a two-page thank you letter reiterating your interest and qualifications, or do you write a handwritten note with a couple of sentences to express your appreciation?

One way to be certain how to communicate best is to ask each interviewer what works for them. At the end of the interview, you could ask, *"I'd like to follow up with you after our conversation today with just a quick note, what's the best way for me to reach you? What media do you use? Do you prefer video, audio, a handwritten note?"* Consider asking that question of everyone you interview with that day.

Having a follow-up strategy is as important as having an interview strategy, for it can distinguish you and make you even more memorable by showing your thoughtfulness and gratefulness, but most importantly, your interest in the position and the company. Email is the most common way today for following up with someone. You can, instead, send a handwritten note, but it's difficult to ensure the recipient will receive it. Not everyone works in an office setting or may not come in frequently enough to check their mail slot or inbox. To navigate around this, some people who prefer to send handwritten notes will take a picture of the card that the note is written on and email it to their interviewer.

There are also video messages that you can leave for people using Vimeo, TikTok, or other platforms to record a 15-second message and email it to the recipient or post it to their Facebook page. You can even create a video message on LinkedIn, where you've already requested the recipient to be a contact.

Have a Transition Strategy

If you've been laid off, or are unhappy at your job, or if you've decided to make a change to pursue a career with purpose in another field or industry, how are you going to have that conversation with your boss or company? Moreover, how are you going to answer that question when a recruiter, HR representative, or the hiring manager asks, *"Why are you looking to leave your current employer and position?"*

We help our clients prepare for their transition with a well-crafted ***Reason for Leaving Statement***, intended to communicate the business reasons leading to their exit from their last employer. The goal of this statement is to provide the interviewer with a simple, positive message that guides the listener from why you left to what you want to do next. The graphic below describes the logical flow that a Reason for Leaving Statement should follow by placing your situation in the proper perspective.

Placing Your Situation in Perspective

Industry

Company

Department

My Situation

Positive

Next
Steps

Here's an example of a Reason for Leaving Statement from one of our clients that shows certainty and confidence in their decision to leave their hospital.

> *"Like many healthcare organizations, my hospital is going through a major restructuring. Due to a recent merger, accounting functions are being combined. This has meant the elimination of many positions, including mine. I am proud of my contributions to the hospital during my years there, and yet I am looking at this as an opportunity to put my strengths and experience to work in a new setting."*

Use the above Reason for Leaving logic flow to help place your own situation in a proper perspective:

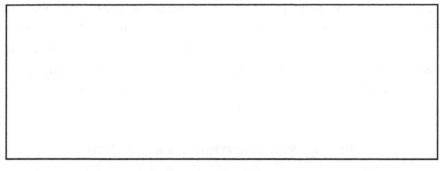

We always coach people before they draft their statement and launch into their search for a position in another organization to first ask themselves, *"How active am I in seeking career development and fulfillment at my current company?"*

Some people are so willing to leave their company believing that the grass is greener on the other side rather than finding a way to make it work where they are. Recall in Chapter 4 how we shared that careers are no longer linear. We don't believe there needs to be a beginning or ending point to a career with predetermined rungs to climb on a fixed-in-position ladder. For many people today, a career journey has more to do with self-discovery and personal fulfillment than it does advancement.

When making a transition, it's really important to be honest with yourself about your reasons for leaving your current situation. You want to be paced and intentional in your thought processes and actions. Don't jump into something that you haven't researched adequately because you feel a compulsion to make a move and leave your present employer.

Your family and friends can be a good sounding board when you're grappling with the notion of a job or career change. However, they will most always be supportive of your reasoning and final decision. It's thoughtful on their part, but not always helpful to you for thinking things through and being certain that you're making the best move.

What is most helpful is meeting and speaking with people who know you and are unbiased and objective in their views. You want to network with business people who are connected to the marketplace, informed in different ways than you, and valuable to you for their advice.

As we noted at the top of this chapter, *interviewing* and *networking* are the two key undertakings that bring your personal brand to life and enable others to learn who you are and what you represent. In the next chapter, you'll discover how networking can do so much more for you if you approach it from the standpoint of mutual benefit, finding connections, earning trust by helping others before asking for help, and by paying it forward.

Questions to Reflect On

1. Which of the mistakes that people make during job interviews do you tend to commit yourself and what actions can you take to correct those errors?

2. When you meet others for the first time, what first impression of yourself do you strive to establish?

3. When sitting down to an interview, what actions do you take at the beginning of the session to show your intent to participate in the process as an equal partner?

4. What is your follow-up strategy after an interview? What do you

strive for in your messaging and format to distinguish yourself from others?

5. Why do you want to work for the prospective employer(s) in your job search? What meaning do you hope to find from those organizations that you're not finding in your current situation?

6. What is your reason for leaving or wanting to leave your current employer and have you prepared a *Reason for Leaving* statement? Have you actively explored other ways that you can find purpose and personal fulfillment with your present employer?

Appendix

Here are two resources to help you best prepare for your interview: The Top Ten Interview Questions that will most likely be asked by recruiters, HR representatives, and hiring managers; and Questions You Should Ask to ensure that the company, its culture, and the position you are interviewing for align with your interests and purpose in work and in life.

The Top Ten Interview Questions

Here are the top ten questions that interviewees typically ask along with tips on how best to respond to each. The most important thing to remember in responding to each of these questions is that you're engaging in a simple conversation between you and another human being. Be open and curious. Assume positive intent in their efforts to try to get to know you better and respond with the same constructive reasons—to have them learn about you.

1. *"Tell me about yourself."*

With this first question, the interviewer is looking to break the ice, but is also looking for an answer that indicates that you're qualified for the position and can respond to an unstructured question. Be relaxed and relatable. This question gives you a chance to tell your story and tie elements back to the position you're interviewing for. For example, maybe you fell in love with the hospitality industry because your grandparents ran a bed and breakfast. Don't be afraid to weave your personality into your storytelling. Know the job description and highlight the most important required skills with relatable stories illustrating your talents and experiences. Keep it short, and be truthful.

2. *"Tell me about your job history."*

Your job history is incredibly important to the interviewer, but so is what you're doing now in the present and what you can bring to them in the future. We find the best approach to answering questions about job history is in a *past-present-future* framework: be brief, direct, and honest about the past; be willing to talk about what you've learned about yourself, how you've grown and honed your skills from the experience; and share what you may potentially do differently in the future to improve upon yourself and your work product. Using a *past-present-future* framework shows that you're reflective and are able to put your actions in greater context. It also shows that you're an agile learner.

3. *"What are your salary expectations?"*
This is where being clear, concise, and direct is incredibly important. First and foremost, you have to know what you're worth. What is the open market for a financial analyst at your level, or a communications manager, a procurement specialist, or an architect? By knowing your worth, we mean not only knowing what you've been paid in the past, but knowing what other companies are paying for that position now so you'll have an understanding of the value that you're bringing them.

Only then can you start answering their "expectations" question with self-assuredness. Don't stress over this one. You can simply handle it by saying, *"This is how much I've made in the past. I would expect my income to be commensurate with the responsibilities I'd be performing. My research tells me that this role is worth up to $90,000."*

We coach our clients to <u>never give a range</u> such as, *"I expect to make somewhere between $60,000 and $90,000 annually."* Guess how they're most likely going to respond? They're going to try to get you for $55,000! Typically, all you'll get from giving an interviewer a range is the low end of the range. You'll fare much better if you respond with, *"I would assume it's worth up to $90,000."* By setting that expectation you might start off at $85 or $80k, but now you're at the top end of whatever range might exist.

Initially in the salary negotiation, it is appropriate at times to provide a salary range. However, as negotiation continues and gets further in the process, we will typically have individuals, once they understand more about the rule, focus on a much tighter range or even a specific number for what they're looking for to do a job.

Often the only chance you're going to get to increase your salary substantially over the course of your career is during the interview process; keep that in mind and be aggressive. If they turn you down if you ask for more than what they're offering, they're most likely not going to rescind the job offer. They're just going to say, *"No, this is what we pay."* Nevertheless, the best time you'll ever have to ask for more money is when you're changing jobs. Negotiate, but be mindful as to when to fold. If they say *"No,"* you have a decision to make. But then again, money shouldn't be the only reason you're wanting to work at that company.

4. *"What is your greatest strength/weakness?"*
When speaking of your strengths, tell short stories that highlight your achievements and, as always, relate your response back to the job. Don't just tell them how you accomplished the feat or overcame the challenge, tell them why it was important and what you learned. Show them that you understand how your role affects the company's business. Explain how your skills and experiences will make their company better.

When speaking to your weaknesses, talk about a real weakness and frame it in a broader, more enlightening perspective:

- How you became aware of your weakness.
- What you're doing to address it.
- How you're holding yourself accountable to improve upon it.
- How it has gotten better for you over time.

If you can remember to apply this framework, you'll have the confidence to share any weakness with believability and genuineness. By acknowledging your flaws and voicing accountability and an intention to rise above them, interviewers will know they can trust that you can and will actually do the work and constantly seek to improve your results.

5. *"How do you want to improve yourself in the next year?"*
When companies are evaluating people for positions, their focus is on whether the person can do the job and their willingness to invest in their

own growth. When asked this question, focus on improving a weakness, building on a strength, or learning a new skill that can help you in your career. Relate your areas of improvement to the role you're seeking, not the role you currently hold.

6. Behavior Questions

The purpose of behavioral questions is for the interviewer to watch the process in which you critically think about things and make decisions. For instance, a scenario posed by the interviewer followed by a question might be, *"Give me a time when you had to implement a change within an organization that you disagreed with, but as a leader, you had to execute anyway? Were you successful in the implementation and what did you learn about yourself?"*

Behavioral questions are all about storytelling and you have to be able to tell an honest, compelling story that lends greater meaning to your experience. The idea here is to convey how present and self-aware you were about your thought processes at the time of your experience, the ultimate decision that you made, and how you confirmed that against your own morals and values. As example, *"I had to lay off 250 people when I thought only two needed to be discharged."* Be open and allow for vulnerability in your awareness of what happened, how you implemented the change, how you overcame the challenges, and how you improved and moved forward.

7. Changing Working Environments

Without question, the pandemic of 2020 changed the structure and place of work. The general question interviewers asked in the midst of the virus was, *"What is your position on working from home?"* Over the course of the past two years, people have become enamored with the ability to work from home and many today are reluctant to give that up. Over that time, they carved out home office space and invested in equipment and technologies to stay connected to their companies and team members. Many altered other aspects of their lives and that of their families in some instances to accommodate working from home.

The pandemic is in the past now and companies are desirous of strengthening their cultures and improving team productivity and sales once again. The question recruiters, HR representatives, and hiring managers are asking now is, *"What is your position on working in an office setting or in a hybrid model of working out of the office and working out of your home?"*

The key is knowing where you stand on this issue and whether you're flexible or not. You have to answer the question honestly for your own well-being. You're interviewing them for a career with purpose, and if that requires you working remotely, then this could be a deal breaker for you. Then again, if you did your homework on the company, you would know where their direction is regarding working environments and what their preferences are. If you're on the fence about it and can go either way, show your flexibility and adaptability by saying, *"I'm happy to look at whatever model you have and figure out what works best for us to work together."*

8. The Add-On Question

You have to be careful with these kinds of questions that are often delivered in a very casual, off-the-cuff way. Sometimes you'll get an add-on just when you think you're building a rapport with the interviewer and feeling confident with everything you've said thus far. The question could come in the form of, *"From what you said earlier, I understand what the team was able to accomplish, but what was your role in that?"*

Don't take it defensively; they're not necessarily trying to trip you up. Perhaps you're just not delivering the story thoroughly enough. There is such a thing as being too concise! Either you're not being clear or they're not understanding in a way that's consistent with what you're saying. Whatever the reason, the question has been asked, so take the stance that you didn't explain it well enough. Let that be your default or else you'll become defensive and lose your calm demeanor and show of confidence. Take a step back, ask any clarifying questions about what they're looking for, and then answer the question. Above all, you have to be consistent and truthful—from your story to your resume to your digital brand presence to the stories you tell in your interviews.

9. *"Why Do You Want to Work Here?"*

If you're advancing in the interview process, it's probably less about your technical skills and more about cultural fit within their company, within a department, or within an existing team. Companies often use this question to measure how excited you are for the position and how committed you are to their mission and products or services.

It's important to remember that your answer to this question should not be about what you're hoping to extract out of the job for yourself. Of course, you want to grow and develop in your career, but it's also about the purpose of the organization and the values that you share with them.

10. The Casual Statement and Long Pause

This is similar to the add-on question where the interviewer may make a very casual statement about something such as, *"All of our salespeople love making cold calls. They sort of make a contest out of it. It's just something that we do. You must know what that's like?"*

Don't get baited into answering that with something as transparent as, *"I love cold calling!"* You have to be very present when statements of this nature are made with an expectation for you to respond. Listen carefully to what they're saying or suggesting or what they're actually asking for. We often find organizations lure interviewees into saying the opposite of what they may have said earlier or had written in their resumes. They're testing to see if they can set an expectation with you or to see how consistent you are with your messaging.

When those kinds of statements are made, we typically instruct our clients to be curious and ask more questions before commenting. For example, *"So, from a cultural standpoint, when you look at success of sales, how many connections do you assume your sales teams should be making on a daily basis?"*

Finally, take notes during interview questions using "quiet" pen and paper. By that we mean don't make a lot of rustling noises or fanfare to impress the interviewer with your notetaking. Taking notes helps you to recall, frame, and ask the most impactful questions at the end of the interview. It also provides content ideas for your follow-up thank you note.

Questions to Ask Interviewers

There is one last question that the interviewer will most always ask of the interviewee, and it will come from the recruiter, HR representative, and hiring manager: *"Do you have any questions for me?"*

Knowing this, you should have pre-planned questions ready and tailored to the person you're speaking with. For instance, it's not productive to ask HR about marketing strategies or a senior leader about the company's dental plan. As an interviewee, you have to be prepared with the kind of questions that address what's most important to you about working for that company.

If you're uncertain if the interviewer is going to ask that one last question, it's a good strategy to say at the beginning of the interview, *"I appreciate your time to get together. I do have a couple of questions that I'd like to ask at the end of our interview if we can secure a few minutes for that. Will that be okay with you?"*

This request immediately allows you to take ownership of the interview or at the very least, show your interest and earnestness. Your intent is to allow space for the interviewer to manage the interview, but you're putting it out there that you're going to have questions. If time doesn't allow for questions at the end of the interview, acknowledge that you didn't have time and ask to set up time to be able to ask those questions.

Here are key questions to ask of each of the three groups of individuals who typically participate in the interview process:

Questions for Headhunters and Recruiters:

1. What did you see on my resume that made you want to meet me today?

2. What do you know about my interviewers? What's their role and their style?

3. What is the company (or hiring manager) looking for specifically?

4. Why have you put me forward for the job?

5. Why is the position open? Why is the company hiring?

Questions for Human Resources:

1. Why do you enjoy working for this company?

2. In your opinion, what's the most important contribution that this company expects from its employees?

3. In your opinion, what is the most important contribution that this company expects from this position?

4. What can you tell me about the company's management style?

5. What do you consider to be the organization's strengths and weaknesses?

Questions for Hiring Managers:

1. How was the incumbent successful in this role, or, why wasn't the incumbent successful?

2. In six months or one year as you look back on this position, what will you want to see to know that I was successful in the execution of my responsibilities?

3. What are the organization's three most important goals?

4. How do you see this position impacting the achievement of those goals?

5. What personal qualities or characteristics do you most value?

8

Networking Is the Secret Sauce

"Seek first to understand, then to be understood."
—Stephen R. Covey

There's no denying that the vast majority of business professionals attend networking events in order to gain something for themselves and their careers. Many will arrive expecting to uncover new job opportunities or sign up new customers for their businesses. Many will show up hoping to strengthen professional business ties or learn new techniques or technologies to get their startups off the ground. Unfortunately, many will leave empty-handed and disappointed with the entire process.

They attend these events with preconceived notions of the purpose of networking and feel pressured to score something for themselves to feel it was a worthwhile use of their time. That perception of networking as hunting and cajoling for opportunities has created such a distaste for the process that it's caused many to underutilize one of their most valuable resources when considering a job or career transition.

A global survey of 16,000 LinkedIn users revealed that while nearly 80 percent of professionals consider networking crucial to career success, almost 40 percent admit that they find it hard to participate.[28] Many will force themselves to attend happy hour meetups and mixers, seminars, breakfast or luncheon meetings, or virtual get-togethers, but don't like the process. They approach it with antipathy because the behaviors required of them feel awkward and unnatural.

Yes, we've seen people leave networking events disheartened and frustrated, but we've also witnessed the exact opposite. Time and again, people walk away with new business relationships and a handful of business cards and notes on how they intend to follow up. They leave feeling inspired and excited over the opportunities they created for others and for themselves.

In our experience, the major difference between these two outcomes is that people who leave on a high note are typically the ones who have moved beyond the singular thought of what's in it for them. Instead, they join in intent on developing new relationships, offering useful advice, and creating connections for others. They must be doing something right. The ones leaving empty-handed are missing out on the fact that 85 percent of available or soon-to-be-available jobs are filled through networking.[29] Most don't realize that before the vast majority of those positions are posted online or listed anywhere, they're already filled either internally or through a referral from someone knowing someone and making a connection.

Networking, in its purest form, is joy in meeting others, being curious about their interests, and expressing your passion for things that interest you. It's an understanding that everyone in the room has value and your intent is to discover what their value is. That is the true meaning and purpose of networking and one that makes it an activity worth engaging in to advance your career while at the same time advancing the careers of others.

At the end of the day, it's not about what you think might happen for you; it's about meeting people and fostering productive relationships. There's no point in going through all of that effort if you're not going to enjoy meeting others and doing something positive for them along the way. And when you least expect it, something great might come along for you, something better than you even planned for.

Our goal in this chapter is to demystify networking and reveal ways to engage with others that will be most productive for you and your business connections. We approach networking as a tactic to empower your job search strategy and to hone continuously the course of your career. Moreover, and remaining true to the theme of our book, our approach to networking is to enable your career to serve your purpose and inspire you to be a part of something bigger, something outside of yourself.

Careering with Purpose

A job search should not be a revolutionary event that rises up with a flurry of activity and suddenly ends the moment you land a position; then several years later, reactivates when you decide or need to job search again. There's a great deal of value, personal discovery, and opportunity lost between these episodes when people choose to approach their careers as a series of unplanned stops and detours, often not under their control.

This is exactly why we approach the word "career" as a verb as reflected in the title of our book. To career is to follow your North Star, knowing that no matter how far you travel, how much time you invest in getting there, or the amount of effort you exert, you'll never arrive at the North Star. Yet, you make continuous adjustments to your compass heading as you encounter different and challenging terrain to ensure you're always on the right path. Similarly, careering with purpose is you guiding yourself toward your aspiration—the person you want to be, doing the work that gives you the greatest sense of fulfillment.

We believe that networking is an enabler of one's purpose and the very best method you can use to nurture and keep your career relevant. If approached with the right intentions along with patience and trust, it becomes a powerful tool for making new connections, cultivating relationships, and creating opportunities for others as well as yourself.

Networking with Purpose

In Chapter 7, we listed the mistakes people most often make when interviewing that can be controlled for with proper foresight and preparation and make all the difference in your outcome. We're going to take a different tack with networking and enumerate the ways in which people correctly and effectively engage with others.

Through our practice, we have identified *The Nine Ways to Network with Purpose* that can make all the difference in the enduring quality of the connections you make and in your chances in finding the job or career that brings you the greatest happiness. There are many tips that we could share with you on how to show up and network with purpose, but these nine continuously surface as the most valuable to remember and practice: (1) network before you need to; (2) be yourself; (3) know your purpose; (4) set aside your personal agenda; (5) be responsible for your own search; (6) follow up and follow through; (7) have patience and trust the process; (8) connect the dots for others; and (9) show humility in all your actions.

The secret sauce is in how you bring these elements together to showcase who you are and what you're capable of. Adopting these nine practices will make you an effective networker and firmly place you in the wheelhouse of your career, deliberate about your bearing, and open to the opportunities that come before you.

1) Network Before You Need To

Given that upwards of 65 percent of all communication is nonverbal, seasoned networkers and people with positions of influence can sense desperation from across the room. People who are new to networking or have a look of "*I need to find a job*" in their eyes are easy to spot and most always seem uncomfortable in their clothes. They emit so much nervous energy that you can almost feel their awkwardness from across the room.

Networkers can also spot those who are in it only for themselves. They're the ones with pens in hand and carrying leather folders overflowing with resumes. The seasoned and influential will avoid them as well so as not to be drawn into a one-sided conversation with someone crowing about their accomplishments.

We have attended enough networking events to fill several lifetimes, so believe us when we say that those two nonverbals of <u>desperation</u> and <u>self-absorption</u> will send other networkers running for cover. People prefer to engage with others who are calm, confident, and thought-provoking; and the only way to communicate that relaxed persona is to network because you want to and not because you need to. Networking when you already have a job and are happily engrossed in your career changes your perspective, and as a result, alters your motives from personal gain to meeting new people and possibly making valuable connections for them.

That "other-orientation" from the moment you walk through the doors communicates an entirely different message to others. Your nonverbals will express a desire to meet people and build relationships. And in time, your intentions and actions will brand you with the reputation of being generous rather than self-serving and worthy of their trust.

2) Be Yourself

Your willingness to be open and honest in your presentation of yourself is critical. When you enter the venue, who are you going to be tonight? One of the reasons people are afraid of networking is because they can't be themselves and feel they have to become someone they think others expect them to be.

Shashi, as example, doesn't feel like her authentic self when she's networking. Being in a room full of people that she doesn't know or doesn't really want to be around makes her feel frustrated and anxious. Shashi, who tends to be more of an introvert, explained to us how she feels pressured to change her personality and become more aggressive in meeting people and asking for favors.

Networking is not a show and you're not on stage. You're there to meet and learn about others and highlight what differentiates you from everyone else. You don't want to be a chameleon but to be genuinely *you* so people can be aware of who you really are. That's the intent of networking. You want to build relationships with people who share your values and align with your purpose. If you're not yourself, you're bound to affiliate with people and organizations that will most likely not prove to be long-term connections for you and can potentially steer you off course and away from your desired career direction.

3) Know Your Purpose

You have to have a plan when you network and the two most important components of that plan are to know your value and to know your purpose. If you don't know your value, you're a rudderless ship bouncing about and easy to spot as someone to avoid. It's essential before you attend any networking event to be very clear on what your talents and skills are as well as the connections you can bring to the table in any networking conversation.

Make it your purpose to network to nurture the relationships you have and to develop new associations. Make it your intention to listen for advice and learn those things that can enhance your career, whether it's a tip on a job opportunity or to discover a new technique that could transform the way you currently do business. That mindset will free you to be yourself and zero in on what you want to achieve during the event.

Part of knowing your purpose is to map out the kinds of questions that you'd like to ask at the networking event. In the appendix at the end of this chapter, you'll find a resource you can use in preparing for and participating in networking events including tips on approaching new people, who best to approach, and conversation starters with open-ended questions that can lead to topics for an extended conversation.

4) Set Aside Your Personal Agenda

As we noted at the onset of this chapter, many people attend network events to meet people they wouldn't normally have access to in order to find a new job or gain a new customer. We believe that a key to networking success is to set aside one's personal agenda and instead enter the event with the mindset of, *"What can I do to help someone?"*

Generosity is a very attractive quality that can be shown in many different ways, especially if you know your value. You can be generous with your knowledge and experience, with your connections, and you can just be helpful to others in any way possible. It's a "giving" quality that people find unique and quite memorable.

We look to Stephen Covey to best define this attribute of networking with purpose through the fifth habit found in his classic, *The 7 Habits of Highly Effective People*. Seeking first to understand, then to be understood, is "Having a frame of mind and heart that empathically listens to others first before seeking to be understood in all human interactions." [30]

If you seek to understand others first, you're more bound to listen before you speak. You'll also tend to ask more questions rather than making statements about yourself and how you see things. You're there at the event first to listen and learn, and asking questions encourages others to speak.

You have to be a naturally curious person to be an effective networker. If you're not innately curious, you can still train yourself to ask questions first and learn to wait patiently for people to ask you questions in return.

5) Be Responsible for Your Own Search

Job and career searchers who are not familiar with the proper ways of networking will often ask for favors from their connections such as, *"If you know of any openings, could you contact me and let me know?"* Or, *"Could you bring my resume to the HR or hiring manager?"* Or, *"Could you make an introduction for me and I'll take it from there?"*

They're inconsiderately transferring the responsibility of their job search to someone else, putting the people they're reaching out to at odds with helping them at all. Recipients of these direct kinds of requests often feel pressured to perform on someone else's behalf. Although they won't show or express their dissatisfaction, they tend to become the most disinterested in helping out because they feel they're being taken advantage of. Additionally, everyone is busy. Your request will get lost or forgotten without some follow-up. Take responsibility for your own job search. Those who network with purpose do the hard work of earning someone's trust first and earning it often before asking for their support.

6) Follow Up and Follow Through

Everyone has a lot going on these days, and once you part company with someone whom you just met at a networking event, they've already moved on to the next thing in their lives. You need to be disciplined in making sure you follow up through the right medium and at the right time, and that you're only doing so to benefit the recipient of your message. *"It was great meeting you Monday evening. Thank you for our conversation. I remember you mentioning a study that you heard about but had a hard time finding. I remember reading that study. Here's a link to it. Best regards."*

Don't follow up asking for help of any kind but instead pick out something in what they shared with you that animated them and gave you a window into their interests or achievements. *"I really liked the way you increased engagement and productivity in your plant. I'd love to hear more about that."* Or, *"Congratulations on your achievement. I know how much that award means to you."*

Being meaningful in your follow-up is being memorable. If you connect with someone at an event, you want to reaffirm to that person that you're interested in them—that you two weren't just ships passing. Show that you were listening and are still interested in what they had to say. Take a moment after meeting each person to make a note on their business card about what was important or interesting to them or something memorable that they said so you'll know what your follow-up message will be.

Keep in mind that anyone can write a thank you note, but following through on whatever was discussed and offered to share on your part, like an introduction to someone, is far more important and impactful. It shows you delivered on your promise and strengthens your brand reputation for being a generous person. Take the time to follow through on the commitments you make and do it in an expeditious way. That's going to become your brand, what you're going to be known for and the most memorable thing you can do for someone.

7) Have Patience and Trust the Process

Patience is one of the most important virtues we can develop within ourselves. When we're patient, we are in direct control of our thoughts and our reactions. We stay composed, regardless of what's happening around us. Through patience, we give ourselves time to choose how to respond to a situation rather than be led by our emotions.

There are many pressures that drive a person to be demanding of their network, foremost of which is their need to see results during a most stressful time in their lives. Nevertheless, you need to establish trust with your network relationships, and having patience allows that trust in you to mature in their eyes. Don't be overly intentional in your follow-up and don't come on too strong. Build and strengthen each connection by letting events take their course and allowing each relationship to grow organically.

Trusting the process is having faith that it's going to work, especially if you've invested your time and treasure in helping to develop the contacts in your network. When you really believe and understand that the true value of networking is in helping others, it will come back to you. Believe in and have patience for that return, and believe that the more you put into your networking and the more you give of yourself, the greater your return will be.

8) Connect the Dots for Others

Once you begin listening to people and learning what they bring to the table and start to align that with what you bring and discover the commonalities, you start to realize how your connections can potentially help each other. Make it your goal when you attend a networking event to not just meet people but to connect them in real time and even afterwards in an email. *"Hi Jim, I thought about our conversation at that meetup a couple of weeks ago and I know someone who might be able to use your services. I'd like to introduce the two of you. Would you be open to that?"*

Part of connecting the dots is knowing how you can be useful. Ask this question of every person you meet, *"How can I help you?"* The magical thing about seeking to be useful is that it places you firmly in a listening mode, curious and deliberate in unearthing information that you can use to lend your advice, expertise, references, or connections.

This changes your whole reason for networking, and it goes back to the first attribute of networking before you need to. The freer you are of the pressures of having to find something for yourself, the more generous you can be with your time in support of others. Unfailingly, more people will become your advocates and all your good work will come back to you in many different ways.

9) Show Humility in All Your Actions

This may be the last of *The Nine Ways to Network with Purpose*, but this quality in people touches all the other practices listed above. Humility is the ability to view yourself objectively as an individual with talents as well as flaws. It's also having the self-esteem to understand that even though you are doing well, you do not have to brag about it.

We can't count the number of times we have attended networking events and find people rattling on about what they've done, or who they know, or where they've been. It demonstrates arrogance, self-interest, and a lack of empathy. That's exactly the opposite of how you want to come across during the event and the impression you want to leave behind.

Another aspect of humility is in how you treat others. People are often so quick to dismiss others as unimportant or ineffective in helping them in their job search because they lack an important title or level of power and influence. Showing humility is never dismissing anyone as being unimportant in any way. The mission of networking is to discover the value each person has. Be fully present with each person you meet and curious with an intent to understand where the commonalities are for forming a relationship. Maintain eye contact with the person you're speaking with and don't look over their shoulder for the next conversation or for someone with a bigger title and more power.

For instance, when you're talking with Betsy at a networking event, she's doing everything but focusing on the conversation she is having with you. Her eyes are constantly searching the room for people of greater stature and importance. In the middle of a sentence, she'll blurt out, *"Just a second, I'll be back. I got to go talk to someone."*

It's a major mistake that people make in networking and those on the receiving end can see right through it. Unfortunately, it's become Betsy's brand. In *Leadership ON PURPOSE*, we wrote at length about how we all have positive or negative shadows that we cast over others; these echoes of ourselves precede us before we enter a room and linger long after we've left.[31]

Although it's important for people to know about your professional successes, sharing that information can be a delicate balance, especially if you're a naturally gregarious and expressive person. Simply inform the other person about what you've been up to in a factual way that provides information about you that they may not have. In Chapter 7, we mentioned using what we refer to as *past-present-future* framework: be brief, direct, and honest about the past; be willing to talk about what you've learned about yourself through those experiences; and share how you intend to build upon your skills and experience in the future. You don't need to bang your drum with superlatives, especially among people who know you and already have a positive impression about you.

These nine foundational behaviors when networking with purpose will make you an effective networker who's actively conscious of the people you're meeting with and supportive of the opportunities that may exist. Practicing these will make all the difference in the enduring quality of your connections and in your success in finding the job or career that brings you the greatest sense of personal fulfillment.

AIR: Advice, Information, Referral

There are three stages that we use as a framework when networking with purpose for planning and pacing your efforts before ultimately seeking a referral from someone. These three stages apply whether you're at a group networking event meeting people for the first time or requesting a one-on-one meeting with someone in your inner circle of professional relationships or with new connections who can potentially bridge you to an ultimate decision maker. To be effective, it's necessary that the three steps are approached sequentially to build trust. We use the acronym AIR to make it easy for you to remember and be principled in your approach: (1) asking for advice; (2) providing information in return; and (3) and asking for the referral once trust is established.

Asking for Advice

It all begins with *why* you're requesting a meeting. Although you're the one looking for a job, put that objective to the side completely. Remember the fourth networking practice of setting your personal agenda aside. Think of it as you interviewing someone about a company's culture or the future of an industry. Be curious, ask for advice, and encourage the people you meet to share their knowledge and experience.

You don't want to mislead them though. You do have to let them know why you're networking, and that can be achieved by having a prepared opening statement and question: *"I understand that you've been with Acme Corporation twenty-two years, and I'm interested in your organization as a place I may want to look to land. Would you be willing to tell me a little bit about your career and why you chose to be there?"*

If you can get someone talking about themselves and you show genuine interest in what they're saying about how their career unfolded or what they're involved in, the more they'll see themselves as a mentor to you. It's also flattering to someone when you ask them for their advice. There's a better chance they'll try to help you in some way, especially if you're a likable person: someone who's approachable and personable, open-minded, and willing to engage with many different types of people.

When you're working with a networking contact, always ask for advice first. Don't make the mistake of transferring your responsibility to them by saying, *"Hi Bob, I know that you know Jennifer in HR at XYZ Company, could you give my resume to her?"*

The request for advice could be, *"Hi Bob, I just rewrote the career summary section of my resume. You know me well. Would you mind taking a look at it? I could buy you a coffee and you could just kind of give me your unbiased opinion of it?"*

You could also ask for advice by saying, *"John, I understand that you work at Acme Corporation. I'm really interested in working there and they have a number of opportunities available now. Would you be willing to have a coffee with me and share your thoughts on the culture there?"*

Once they've agreed to sit down with you, respect where they've come from and honor their tradition and history. Don't assume that you know everything. Even if you do know something they don't, listen instead of interjecting. People that you're networking with may have had a more diverse career experience than you. They may even have walked in your shoes at one time. Pay attention and absorb as much of their wisdom as you can, especially of the older members in your network.

Thank them for their willingness to share their time with you. Most important, and this goes back to the likability factor, smile, maintain eye contact at all times, and show your personality. Your facial expressions are a window to your heart and your thoughts. Show them the kind of person you would be to work with.

Providing Information in Return

Asking for advice is so important, but when you're networking, your first intent upon receiving that advice is to do something for that person before you would ever ask them to do something for you. You have to believe that if you do good deeds in your life that you're going to get good things back in return. Those are seeds that you have to plant, and once you've planted a seed with someone, you have to water it and give it light. Stay in contact with them and let them know from time to time that you're thinking of them and that you remember what they talked about that was most valuable and interesting to them.

Before you ask for a referral or an introduction, give something of substance and relevance to the life or career of the person who just had that coffee with you. It could be a book, free access to an online subscription, or a link to that study they mentioned having a hard time finding. Your goal is to stand out from others, and following up with that person will make you noteworthy in their minds. Providing information in return for their advice will also show that you were listening and that you valued your time together.

Your affability, generosity, and patience will ultimately pave the way for a follow-up conversation where you can then directly ask for their assistance. But don't rush it. Trying to speed up the process will make all your actions from day one appear contrived and shallow. The intent of seeking advice first and then providing information in return is to build trust over time so that you've earned the permission to ask for their support or advocacy in the future.

Asking for the Referral

Consider your building of trust as savings in a bank account that you're setting aside to be able to pay for the referral down the road. As we shared at the onset of this chapter, networking is about fostering relationships first, and if you haven't set a solid foundation and begun building a relationship, you have no business in asking that person for a referral.

Assuming you have built that relationship and you have plenty of savings in your account, asking for that referral can take many forms with email being the most prevalent medium that's personal and formal. Your communication could be, *"Thanks for the conversation we had the other day. I just noticed that there's an opening in accounts payable at XYZ. Would you be comfortable in letting me know who the hiring manager is for that department?"*

Your request for a referral or introduction could be very direct, depending on the relationship you've built. If it's strong enough, you could ask, *"Could you please forward my resume that I sent you to the hiring manager for the accounts payable department?"*

When seeking a referral, it's important not to assume that the person is going to refer you, or introduce you, or advocate for you. Many will worry about their reputation for referring someone whose personality or work culture may not click with a manager or with a team, even though that person may have the skills and experience to do the job. Make certain that you're comfortable with the person you're requesting a reference from and that they're comfortable referring you. To be certain and non-presumptuous, you could ask, *"Are you comfortable with giving me a referral?"*

The bottom line is you have to ask permission, but you have to have earned the right to do so. Be patient and take the time to nurture the relationship. You may never ask your most important business relationships for a referral, but it shouldn't stop you from keeping them in your inner circle and maintaining those relationships. You may be able to help someone else with your connections.

Learn How to Read a Room

One area we certainly want to address in this chapter on networking is knowing how to read a room. Reading a room is having a sensitivity for the emotions and thoughts of those present, especially in determining what would be appropriate or inappropriate for you to say or do. It's about tuning in to and being actively conscious of what's going on around you—the people, the setting, your role in it, and what it means.

When attending a networking event, it's always best to go with another person who has a job, loves what they do, and thinks highly of you. That's the ultimate companion! You can introduce them to the people you meet and you'll know they'll be saying positive things about you if you part company. It always makes networking much easier and much more fun when you walk into a room with someone else. It's not about having that other person as a safety blanket, but rather, it presents you as an active person and keeps your energy level high.

If you do go alone, you can look for the host or someone that you know and ask them to introduce you to people whom you're interested in meeting. Your request could go something like this:

"Hey Susan, I want you to meet someone. Janice and I are business associates and have become friends over the years. She hails from your hometown and went to the University of Wisconsin-Madison. I know you're an alumnus there. There's all kind of similarities between you two. I think you might enjoy talking with each other a bit and seeing if there are any shared experiences in there somewhere!"

Look for small groups and be willing to walk up to them with a pleasant, inquisitive countenance about you. When you walk up to two people in a meeting, don't close the triangle making it difficult for someone else to join in. Instead, stand at the side of either one of the two people in order to leave open room for a fourth to enter the conversation.

You could also look for individuals who are standing alone; people who you know have connections and would be willing to talk, but may be too shy to initiate conversations. Gravitate toward them first to draw them in. Make it easy for them to talk with you by showing genuine interest in them and asking follow-up questions.

Arm yourself with a few conversation starters (see the appendix at the end of the chapter for ideas) and look for the chance to make a few friends. You should always have something prepared to answer the inevitable, *"So what do you do?"* Be concise and don't be too long-winded in your response. Leave room for the other person to ask about the details in your short story that interest them.

You can start a conversation by asking simple questions that leave room for a response. However, easy questions such as, *"Are you enjoying yourself?"* can break the ice but don't encourage the discussion to continue. Instead, once you've introduced yourself, you could ask, *"What company do you work for?"* Then, *"How do you like it there?"* invites them to talk about their company, what they do, and what interests them. Your questions will reveal something of interest and value to them that you can refer to in your follow-up after the event.

Regional Mindfulness

The art of networking—from introducing yourself, to asking for advice, to responding to questions asked of you doesn't work the same everywhere. You have to be aware of cultural differences and expectations, especially when you take into consideration the different regions of the United States, let alone different regions in the world.

Using a subtle, deliberate, thoughtful approach to networking may work best in the Midwest, but use that style in New York and you may not gain much traction. Northwesterners, although very giving people, tend to be very direct and abrupt in their conversations.

While networking in New York City, James, a director of sales for a large company in the Midwest, was told by a representative of a prospective employer whom he had just met, *"Have you given any thought about becoming a national sales rep for our firm?"*

It wasn't what James had in mind at the time, so he replied in a measured way by saying, *"Well, that's an interesting idea. I'd like to give that some thought."*

Although James was immediately animated by the thought of a national sales representative position the moment it was presented to him, he didn't come across that way to the company representative and the job was offered to someone else. James wasn't being declarative enough for the kind of role he wanted in that part of the country. He could have revealed his true feelings right at that meeting by saying, *"This is something I think I could really excel in. Sounds interesting!"*

Being outspoken and dynamic in your networking is expected in the Northeast, but not so much in the South. In that part of the U.S., interactions are more paced and tend to center on how well you're connected to the history of the company or its employees. *"Our fathers used to work together at the paper mill."* Or, *"My grandmother dated your grandfather."* In the South, it's all about legacy, and in legacy, people are able find a reason for having confidence and trust in someone.

The West and Northwest have their characteristics as well. The West is very casual and laid back. Life is less harried and people will have more time for you. But keep in mind that things don't move that quickly either. In the Northwest, it may be a question of whether you're involved with the right social causes. Being able to speak to different facets of your background, such as your volunteerism and community outreach efforts, can have as much importance as your talents, skills, and experience.

Maintaining Your Network

Growing a professional network takes time and you have to be careful and disciplined so as not to get complacent with your connections. It could be a full-time job just staying in touch with all the people you've networked with or have become connected with over the course of your career, but there will be several that you may not want to lose touch with. You need to make sure that every once in a while you reach out to them, even if simply to ask how things are. Networking is all about maintaining and strengthening relationships over time.

How do you decide who to maintain connections with? We suggest that you create a Network Contact Strategy that has, at its core, your Inner

Circle of friends and associates. These are the people who really know you well, and that you can fail in front of with no fear or embarrassment. They're the people that you have a purpose-based connection with and the ones that you trust and can rely on. This inner circle, as illustrated in the graphic below, should be your priority in maintaining connections.

Your Network Contact Strategy

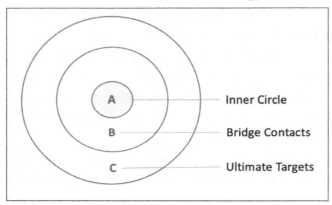

Your B connections are your bridge contacts, those who can connect you to other people, namely, your C contacts, the decision makers who can potentially hire you; they are your ultimate target. What parallels our definition of inner circle and bridge contacts are your connections on LinkedIn where you'll find your first-, second-, or third-degree connections.

First-degree relationships **are people** you are directly connected to by having either accepted their invitation to connect or them having accepted yours. Second-degree connections are people who are connected to your first-degree connections while third-degree people are connected to your second-degree connections.

Bridge contacts, or second-degree connections in LinkedIn parlance, are where the power of your network truly resides. These are the people that you can reach out to directly and suggest, *"I came across your profile and thought it was interesting that we have a number of things in common. I'd love to connect and get to know you a bit better and see how I can possibly help you."*

Realize that it may take several bridge connections before you get to that ultimate decision maker. Accept also that you'll never know how long that bridge will extend until you're on it and developing those contacts. You have to step onto that bridge though, and you're firmly there each time you network with an intention to connect the dots.

Have a Functioning BS Radar

When networking, you need to have an internal radar that is constantly on and sweeping for people whose intention is to only draw energy and time away from you. You have to fine-tune your sensitivity to detecting when someone is trying to work you versus being really in it for the relationship, and some of the tips we shared in this chapter will help you accomplish that. It gets easy to waste time on people who attend networking events to achieve personal goals only and give nothing in return.

On the other side of the coin, you don't want to appear as "that person" on someone else's BS radar! Walk in with purpose and your nonverbals communicating a calm confidence and a desire to meet people and build relationships.

Paying It Forward

The idea of "paying it forward" is simply performing acts of kindness with no intention of ever receiving something in return. For example, paying for the meal of the car behind you in the drive-through or being a pro bono guest lecturer at a local university. There are many doctors, psychologists, lawyers, and coaches who offer their services entirely for free to those who are in need.

In the context of networking, paying it forward is giving back for all the support and opportunities that came your way over the years. For instance, in the beginning of your professional career, your network was small and you didn't have the experience to be a mentor to someone coming up. As you progressed in your career, your network became larger, built from years' worth of experience and interactions.

Now it's your turn to pay it forward. You can *become* a coach, or mentor, or simply a trusted advisor to someone early in their career, or strug-

gling now after being downsized, or looking for something more meaningful in their lives. Your advice and connections can be invaluable to them.
Ask yourself, who in your network would benefit from an introduction? If
you feel like two people should be connected with each other and you're
confident in your referral, then open doors for them and pay it forward.

Questions to Reflect On

1. Of the *Nine Ways to Network with Purpose*, which one or more
    best illustrates your approach to networking?

2. How would people describe your reputation as a networker?
    What makes you memorable?

3. Is it your practice to network without being in a job search your-
    self? How would you explain your purpose? What changes have
    you noticed take place in your attitude and the ways you engage
    with others?

4. What types of conversation starters do you use to make it easier
    for other networkers to meet you for the first time?

5. What methods do you use to get others to talk about themselves?
    What mental devices do you use to remember people's names?
    What's your method for remembering what each contact said?

6. In what ways do you pay it forward? Upon reflection, who in
    your network of inner circle relationships and bridge contacts can
    you connect the dots for and help make a positive difference in
    their work life?

Appendix

Tips on Participating in Network Events

Here's a quick resource to use in preparing for and participating in networking events including tips on approaching new people, who best to approach, and a useful range of topic areas for conversation starters. Remember, you're networking to have fun and meet new people, not to push your agenda. You want to learn more about the people who are in attendance and discover the ways to connect them to each other.

Tips on Approaching New People:
- Be interesting. Come prepared to discuss events and avoid polarizing discussions. First impressions have been shown to last for months and affect an individual's conclusions. Present yourself with energy, enthusiasm, and a smile.

- Not everyone is okay with shaking hands. It's not the Old West so you can be a little slower on your draw. Be prepared to take their lead but be ready to shake so make sure your right hand is free. Carry drinks, especially cold drinks, in your left hand.

- Name tags are great conversation starters in themselves and should be worn above the pocket on the right side of your shirt, blouse, or blazer.

- Catch the person's eyes and say your name with a smile. You could introduce yourself with, *"Hi, I'm [first/last name], I'm glad to meet you. And you are?"*

- Remember names and ask for someone to repeat their name if you don't hear it.

- Speak clearly, don't mumble, and speak at a reasonable pace and volume. Use the person's name when you're talking with them. This can help you remember their names.

Who Best to Approach:

- Approach people who are on their own. They are likely looking for someone to talk with.

- Also approach two people who are not directly facing each other and create a threesome by introducing yourself to both. You're already connecting the dots!

- Join groups that have gaps in them and are open to new people joining. Listen attentively.

- If you are speaking with someone and another person approaches, introduce yourself, make them feel welcome too.

Conversation Starters:

A conversation starter is an introduction for someone you'd like to speak with to chat with you. An opener often takes the form of an open-ended question, which can lead to topics for an extended conversation. A closed-ended question on the other hand *("Nice weather today, isn't it?")* is less effective because it can be answered with a simple *"Yes,"* which is essentially the end of that conversation!

Here is a useful range of topic ideas with open-ended questions as conversation starters. Opening statements and not questions can be followed by, *"I'm [first/last name], I'm glad to meet you. And you are?"*

The Occasion: *"Hi. What's your connection to this event?"*
Ask a Question: *"Hi. Are you a member or visiting as I am?"*
Positive Self-Revelation: *"I'm glad I didn't eat lunch. The food looks great!"*
The Location: *"What a great place,"* or *"What great food,"* or, *"Wasn't that speaker amazing?"*

Listening:

- Listen actively so you can remember the person and the message and concentrate on what's being said.

- Ignore what's going on behind you or across from you when

you're in a conversation with someone. Sustain eye contact with that person, nod and smile to let them know they're acknowledged and that you're following closely what they're saying.

- It's most important not to monopolize the discussion with your own agenda. Listen more than talk. And when you do speak, keep it brief and positive.

- Once you've listened and made connections between their story and yours or someone you know, a powerful question to ask of them and ultimately everyone you meet at the networking event is, *"How can I help you?"*

9

Title Isn't Everything

*"One cannot choose wisely for a life unless he dares to listen to himself,
his own self, at each moment of his life."*
—Abraham H. Maslow

From the time we scan online job banks, classifieds, or message boards for that first job out of school or for the next level of income or authority at our place of work, we become very attached to job titles.

Titles are so much a part of who we are as people. We are hierarchal in nature and titles are symbolic of our drive to achieve and succeed. Titles are so ingrained in the business landscape now that we've been conditioned to measure our success in terms of those labels, which at times can mislead us over the course of our careers. Add to that, many people equate title with money, benefits, and some level of power and authority. However, title success does not always correlate to financial success or to one's ability to influence.

There are people who have vice president or executive director titles who work in non-profit organizations and take home less than most managers do in for-profit companies. Then again, we also know presidents of non-profits who are well-paid for the work they do. It's a matter of understanding the meaning and distinction of titles across industries and within types of businesses to know what you're in for and what you're getting out of the position for yourself.

In the financial services industry, a senior vice president in a bank can have similar in authority to a senior manager in a manufacturing organization. In family-based companies, hierarchies tend to be very flat and senior level positions of authority and decision making are often held by or reserved for family members.

Be cautious of titles for they aren't always as they appear. Organizations often use or inflate titles to attract candidates or keep key employees from leaving, although the authority, pay, and benefits are often not commensurate with the title. The candidate for a title could reside in any functional area of an organization such as law, marketing, finance, or operations. For instance, we know many directors of human resources who believe they've put in the time and are now ready to be vice presidents. They'll leave their corporations and accept positions in small companies dangling VP or CHRO titles when all those small entities want out of the new hires is their corporate process knowledge and not strategic understanding or planning. Unfortunately, when that director who is now a vice president takes their next career step, their resumes and stories will only reflect the skills and experience of a manager of HR processes and not those of a strategic HR leader.

Title does not always equate to scope and responsibility. You could be a director and have a great deal more strategic responsibility in a company than as a vice president in another. Many people looking to change jobs or careers end up chasing titles and are not accumulating the skills and experience along their career journeys that will ultimately serve their career purpose in the long run.

Title inflation also has a lot to do with the expectations people place on themselves and the progress they're making in their careers. Those expectations are often reflected in the titles they embellish on their resumes. Without the proper responsibilities to have earned their labels, many people find themselves over their heads when attempting to leverage that title into a future position in another organization.

Our intent in this chapter is to help you see "title" through a different lens as you career with purpose. In some instances, titles can be very useful for accomplishing your objectives, but people can often be lured by titles and find themselves caught up in a quest where title, not purpose, is defining and directing their careers.

Put Title in Perspective

What are your assumptions about what a greater job title will provide you? People most often think of salary, stock options, and benefits. For others, it's status and authority; the power to manage people and make decisions. Some anticipate greater job satisfaction foreseeing their involvement in more strategic work and contributing at a higher level. Some imagine greater social acceptance and respect from others.

As you evaluate positions and opportunities for advancement that cross your path, put title in perspective. It's a mistake to believe that title will define and represent everything for you, for what comes with the titled position is equally if not more important. To ensure that the job and career choices you make are centered on your needs and aspirations, take the time to determine if (1) the position, (2) your work product, and (3) the culture of the organization are in alignment with your career purpose.

1) Is the Position on Your Path?

What career trajectory do you or will you have as a result of the position? Does it open up doors or avenues for you to continue to grow along your ideal career path, or is it a stopping point? Some organizations may offer an enticing title, but it might mean that you'll be carrying it for a number of years due to the lack of upward or lateral mobility in that organization. As part of your assessment of the company and its industry, make sure there are other avenues for you to grow and develop. A metaphor we often use is to not chase squirrels and stray from your path, because once you're off your path, you'll find it difficult to get back on. Those small meals may end up consuming you by clouding your thinking or distracting you from other opportunities that are more aligned with your long-term career goals.

Recall the story earlier in our book of Susan, the highly paid, successful in-house attorney in the banking industry? She grew frustrated after a couple of years over the legal remit process and was enticed by a company in the same industry to join them as vice president of business development. In a short time, Susan discovered that her new role involved selling banking services and managing client relationships. She found herself adding no value nor learning any new, marketable skills.

What truly unsettled Susan was that she was no longer challenged intellectually as she was as an attorney. She was also off her path of one day providing low to no cost legal services to disadvantaged single mothers.

Susan is now considering leaving the banking industry altogether and trying to restart her legal profession elsewhere.

Be strategic in your approach as you design your career path, then try not to stray from that path. In that fashion, whether you're hierarchical or not, the choices you make and the positions that you'll seek out and accept will always be deliberately thought through and in alignment with your purpose.

A parallel to designing your career path is found in *Leadership ON PURPOSE,* by Michael Grubich and Shelley Smith.[32] In it, the authors illustrate a culture-shaping process that begins with the behaviors of an organization's leaders. When building the culture of an organization toward a desired outcome—a different reality than what currently exists—leaders have to begin with the end in mind, then to lead by example. When employees start experiencing something different, it will influence their beliefs. The change in their beliefs will then lead to them demonstrating different behaviors that are more in line with what is desired and needed in order to achieve the end result.

In a similar way, your career path should be leading to your "end in mind," and the experiences you encounter along the way are there to strengthen your beliefs, guide the actions you take, and confirm the decisions you make. Stay true to that end in mind. The path may sometimes feel unsure and the journey will seem to take longer than it should, but the end result will be more in line with what you ultimately want out of your career.

Stay on your path. However, if you continue to be attracted to experiences that may draw you in other directions, especially if there's a pattern in those distractions, take the time to assess what those signs are telling you. Understand that your career path will be dynamic and should evolve as new experiences come into focus over the course of your work life and shape your beliefs and values. Be open to those changes in you, in your work environment, and in your marketplace.

A career is an evolutionary process as the purpose of work changes throughout your life. You'll find that over the course of that journey, title may matter less as your purpose becomes more defined and prominent in what you do each day.

2) Clarify What the Title Requires and Enables

We have often found that the responsibilities of a titled position in an organization have a lot to do with its traditions, values, and norms. It's incumbent upon you to gain clarity on the roles and responsibilities of the position advertised. If the job title is vice president, what are you VP of? Do you have P&L responsibility? Whom do you report to and whom do they report to? Do you have actual authority to impact or affect operations or policy in a specific way? How much independence will you have in your decision-making?

You should surface these and other questions during the interview process that we spoke of in Chapter 7. It is clearly to your benefit to interview the hiring company for the same reasons they're interviewing you. Ask the questions that will help you determine if the role is the right fit for you, keeps you on your career path, and gives you the skills and experience you need to progress. It doesn't matter if you're seeking the role of president, vice president, director, supervisor, or manager. Make sure that you understand the context of the role and your ability to be successful in that position. Look critically at the scope of work, external expectations, and your financial and people-reporting responsibilities. An impressive title won't be worth much when you're looking for your next role and you haven't earned the critical experiences compared to others vying for the same position.

3) Do You Align with the Culture?

In some organizations, if you're not moving up, you're moving out. That kind of culture doesn't work for a lot of people, and those who stick it out are forced to play that game if they hope to survive and be gainfully employed. Not all people are wired that way from a competitive standpoint, and for those who are spirited and driven in that fashion, the vast majority would prefer to be competitive externally, not internally with their peers, teammates, and friends.

Hold out for the kind of culture that you feel most comfortable with. Seek out a culture whose beliefs and values align with yours, but will also allow you to set your own career path and grow and develop in ways that align with *your* beliefs and values. Confirm that the person you report to is well thought of and willing and capable of helping to promote you and whatever career direction you choose to pursue. If your intent is to not seek promotion, make sure that the company provides access to training and development that will allow you to move laterally and create more of a portfolio of career experiences that we spoke of in Chapter 4 instead of a hierarchical resume of the titles you've acquired.

A Career Hierarchy of Needs

Abraham Maslow's "Hierarchy of Needs" is a theory of psychology explaining human motivation based on the pursuit of different levels of needs. The theory states that humans are motivated to fulfill their needs in a hierarchical fashion. This order begins with the most basic needs being met first before moving on to more advanced needs.[33]

Self-actualization tops Maslow's hierarchy and refers to the desire within us to reach our full potential. According to Maslow, this need can only be met once all of the other basic needs are satisfied. While Maslow's theory is generally portrayed as a hierarchy, Maslow noted that the order in which these needs are fulfilled does not always follow a standard progression.

Paralleling Maslow's hierarchy, we have created a *Career Hierarchy of Needs* where career fulfillment can only be achieved once all of the other career needs are met, beginning with knowing yourself and your purpose. Just as with Maslow's hierarchy, one's career hierarchy does not necessarily follow a standard progression. As we shared earlier, your career path will evolve as new experiences come into focus over the course of your work life and advance your beliefs and values. You'll find that in our *Career Hierarchy of Needs*, title does not define or satisfy your full potential.

Career Hierarchy of Needs

```
                    Career
                  Fulfillment
                  ────────────
                  Recognition
                ────────────────
                    Culture
              ────────────────────
                    Content
            ────────────────────────
                    Purpose
```

In our *Career Hierarchy of Needs*, the first level that must be satisfied is knowing your **Purpose**, what meaning you want to derive from your work, and what you desire to accomplish in your work life. We believe that is the foundational need that must be met if you hope to be on the path to attaining career fulfillment.

The **Content** of the position is the next need that must be addressed. What will you be doing that aligns with your purpose, your story, and your brand? Is your daily effort going to give you job satisfaction? Many people give only a second thought, if any thought at all, to the content of the job. Title and compensation tend to come first in their minds. As we've shared earlier, titles can be misleading and they may not afford you the ability to grow in your skills and experience. The content has to be there for you to find fulfillment and enjoyment in what you do for a living.

Having satisfied the needs of knowing your purpose and being engaged in work that allows you to develop in alignment with that purpose, the next is to be in a work **Culture** that shares your values and supports your growth and development in whatever direction you choose to take.

Having purpose, working at what makes you happy, and working with others who share your values and interests satisfy the basic needs for a fulfilling career. Continuing the parallel to Maslow's hierarchy, once the needs at the bottom three levels have been satisfied, the esteem needs begin to play a more prominent role in motivating behavior. At this level, it becomes increasingly important to gain the respect and appreciation of others. People have a need to accomplish things, then have their efforts recognized. From a *Career Hierarchy of Needs,* once the bottom three levels have been satisfied, self-esteem and **Recognition** for one's efforts would be found in title, compensation, and benefits. There's nothing wrong with having self-esteem and seeking recognition and respect, but in the end, it's not your title but what you do that defines you and brings you the greatest satisfaction.

Once you've satisfied these needs, you will have attained *Career Fulfillment* in parallel to Maslow's stage of self-actualization or becoming everything that you are capable of becoming. You will be in a career that has meaning and enables you to express who you are and what you value through your work effort. You are working at what you love and believe in. Nevertheless, there has to be a constant vigil, as we shared in Chapter 2, of looking inward to confirm exactly what you want out of your work life; looking outward, to assess the growth potential of your company, industry, and marketplace; and looking forward, to plan out the things you want to achieve in that one-third of your life spent working at something meaningful. That is the hierarchy of things that, in the long run, will bring you the greatest sense of career fulfillment.

Are Your Minimum Expectations Being Met?

One of the most prevalent approaches to determining job satisfaction is Frederick Irving Herzberg's "Two-Factor Theory." Influenced by Maslow's Hierarchy of Needs, Herzberg conducted a series of studies attempting to determine what factors in work environments cause job satisfaction or dissatisfaction.[34]

Herzberg's theory argues that job satisfaction and dissatisfaction have their own set of factors and are independent of each other. This is contrary to the generally held belief that job satisfaction is dependent upon the things that cause job dissatisfaction. Herzberg proposes that the factors that contribute most to job satisfaction are motivators such as achievement, recognition, the work itself; and responsibility and opportunities for advancement and growth; and that the factors that contribute most to job dissatisfaction are work relationships, supervisor relationships, working conditions, and salary.[35]

As an exercise, let's use Herzberg's Two-Factor Theory to assess your current job, evaluate a new position in your organization, or assess a position in a different company. What are your *Job Satisfiers*, those elements that are above and beyond your minimum expectations? These could be the content of your job, your ability to learn and develop new skills, the people that you work with and friendships that you've developed, or reporting to a great manager.

Next, what are your *Job Dissatisfiers*? These are the minimum expectations that are not being met in your current job or the position you're vying for. These are your non-negotiables, the factors that must exist or must not exist in order for you to stay in your job or say yes to a new position. What tops this list for you? Examples of dissatisfiers are factors such as having to work for a bad manager, not receiving a salary commensurate with your workload, not having hybrid working options, or a benefits package that doesn't meet your needs or the needs of your family.

Job Satisfiers	**Job Dissatisfiers**
maximum expectations	*minimum expectations*
that you receive	*that you don't receive*

If you're using this exercise to assess your current job, think through and list your dissatisfiers and measure them against your satisfiers. Then step back and ask yourself, *"Am I leaving for the right reasons?"* If you are, then cataloging these non-negotiables and desirables will help give you direction and guide your decisions. Moreover, if you're using this exercise to evaluate a new position of interest, are you pursuing it for the right reasons and are you assured that you're going to get what you want? Do your satisfiers outweigh your dissatisfiers?

Think Long-Term

Our closing thought on title not being everything is a perspective that we encourage clients in our practice to adopt, and that is to think long-term about your career. You don't want to day-trade your career by buying into and out of titles as a way to grow. Many people are focused so intently on short-term goals and gains that they have totally neglected their longer-term and deepest dreams, visions, and goals.

If you're working at your job or looking for a job, don't singularly focus on what you're getting right now or allow yourself to be completely distracted and drawn off path by the squirrel you're chasing. Focus on the long-term implications. View the bigger and broader picture. What are the career options for you down the road? What's happening with the company or the industry that you're in? Will a job change ultimately require moving to another part of the country or the world? How does your decision affect you and your family if you have one or plan on having one? How does it affect your spouse's career path? Will your children have to change high schools and lose friendships or scholarship opportunities?

In *Leadership ON PURPOSE*, Mike Grubich and Shelley Smith designate Systems Thinking as one of the Six Attributes of Agile Leaders.[36] In their book, they shared how the best leaders are seen as acting in the best interests of the organization as a whole. They tend to view the organization from a broader perspective, seeing overall structures, patterns, and cycles, rather than only specific functions or events.

We believe systems thinking is an appropriate parallel for reflecting long-term about your career. In order to build a happy and successful life, you have to not only focus on what's necessary to sustain you in the immediate future (financially and otherwise) but also continually plant the seeds for who and what you wish to be and to become. Having a long-term view of your career is motivating and guiding, and makes it far more likely you'll succeed.

Questions to Reflect On

1. What are your assumptions about what a greater job title could provide you?

2. When is title important and worth pursuing?

3. Have you in your career accepted a position based on title and found it wasn't what you expected? What did you learn from that experience?

4. When job searching, what steps do you take or guidelines do you follow to make sure your career choices are centered on your long-term needs and aspirations and not on chasing short-term squirrels?

5. If you were to create your own *Career Hierarchy of Needs*, how similar or dissimilar to the ones presented in this chapter would your levels of needs be?

6. When assessing your Job Satisfiers and Job Dissatisfiers from the exercise above, what action can you take to either create new satisfiers or bring a dissatisfier up to minimum expectation?

10

Secrets for Effective Salary Negotiation

"Self-worth comes from one thing—thinking that you are worthy."
—Dr. Wayne W. Dyer

Larry worked hard at his new role on the project team and the results showed it. In the past year, the startup had expanded its client base and the larger software companies were taking notice. Larry was anxious to ask for a raise. He was so grateful for the job offer that he made the mistake of not asking for enough during the interview process when they asked about his salary requirements. He was confident that the position was worth a significantly higher salary, especially given his contribution to the company's successful year. He wasn't going to be satisfied with the standard 3-5 percent increase. He went in with his list of accomplishments and knowledge of comparable positions in the marketplace and he got them to raise his base by 13 percent.

Meg, who works in higher education, received an offer for $50,000, which is standard for the role she would be filling. She was happy to receive the offer, but she wasn't just going to accept it as is and asked if they could increase it by five thousand dollars. The most they could offer her was $52,000, which she accepted, but she was also able to negotiate a relocation bonus of $2,000, which brought her closer to her compensation goal for her first year.

When the company declined Gail's counteroffer on salary, she countered back by asking for a relocation expense that would include a moving expense, temporary housing and expenses while she and her family looked for a new home, the employer covering closing costs, and two weeks additional vacation time, all of which the company agreed to. These examples demonstrate the value of negotiating. A change in job is always the best time (and sometimes the only time) to negotiate an increase in base salary.

Why You Should *Always* Negotiate

You may love the idea of negotiating, or like many, abhor having to haggle over anything, even something as important as income. Nevertheless, research and experience have proven time and again that taking the initiative to negotiate effectively is worth your effort.

While not wanting to pay more than necessary, most employers are prepared expect to pay more than their initial offer. In our experience, many employers would have paid more for their new hires if they had simply asked. A majority of employers in the U.S. (73 percent) say they would be willing to negotiate salary on an initial job offer. Yet, more than half of workers (55 percent) do not even ask for a higher salary when offered a new position.[37]

Employers expect you to negotiate. It indicates to them that you won't shy away from negotiating on behalf of the organization. Their thinking is, if the candidate is going to fight for themselves, they're more likely to have it in them to fight for the company. There's something very real and palpable about that reasoning. If you're not willing to fight for something that's important to you, you may not have it in you to fight for anything else.

What is the value that you place on yourself and the work that you do? You have to believe in your worth. Think about negotiating your salary just as you would give consideration to all the other factors that we've presented in this book including finding happiness and satisfaction in your work life and being a part of a culture that shares your values. Being fairly compensated for your work product is one of those factors. If you're not happy with your salary, you're going to start off on the wrong foot. Knowing that employers are anticipating you asking for more, make sure that you are comfortable with how you are being compensated and that you're not leaving anything on the table. You don't want salary to be a distraction that causes you to undercommit and underperform.

Jeffrey was in the final stages of interviewing for a new job and had his target salary range in mind. When the hiring company called to present their salary offer, Jeffrey felt it was a little less than what he was hoping for. Yet, he accepted the offer on the spot. He was so excited about what he would be doing and immediately rationalized that the money didn't matter as much as the job itself. Jeffrey liked the manager he would be working for, the commute was shorter, and there would be far more work flexibility in this job compared to the last. The salary was not where he wanted it to be, but everything else was agreeable to him.

One Friday evening after work, Jeffrey was out having drinks at the local watering hole with a couple of his co-workers and discovered that they were making more money than he was doing the same job. The gap wasn't all that great but what gap there was began to irritate him and grow wider in his mind than it actually was. He didn't take the opportunity to negotiate for more as some of his teammates did when the salary offer was initially made to them.

It bothered Jeffrey to the point where he met with his manager and claimed that he should be making more for the work he was doing. The manager explained to Jeffery that he had the opportunity to negotiate his salary before he was hired and that he would have to wait until his annual performance review to expect any increase. His manager explained that Jeffrey could also work to be promoted, although others with more senior-ity would stand a better chance. Even though the difference wasn't that great, Jeffrey knew that he was going to be behind his peers in income unless he did get a promotion, which didn't seem likely at this company in the near future.

Companies tend to give the amount that you're asking, as long as it's not unrealistic and you have data to substantiate your request. Accord-ing to Fidelity's 2022 Career Assessment Study, 87 percent of professionals ages 25 to 35 who countered on salary, other compensation, or benefits got at least some of what they asked for.[38]

Most people aren't going to ask for 30 percent more in salary; they're going to ask for two or three percent. Why you should negotiate has every-thing to do with your belief in what you're worth and sometimes what others might think you're worth. There are many times when people get offered a salary or compensation package that's at or above their expectations and they immediately rationalize that there's no reason to negotiate any further.

But given that employers expect you to negotiate and are most likely holding back a couple of percentage points on salary or not offering sign-on incentives unless you ask for them, why not take the time, research the offer, and ask the questions that will most likely increase your total compensation?

This chapter is intended to provide a framework for thinking and acting with the purpose of improving your comfort and confidence so you can be more effective in your salary negotiations and ensure that you've maximized your total compensation package. You will find helpful guidance and tools to manage salary questions, analyze your offers, and create a strategy for negotiating all the factors involved in accepting a job offer. We have even provided scripts as a starting place from which to begin crafting your own questions and responses.

Ground Rules for Success

If your goal is to make as much as you can and not leave anything on the table, there are three ground rules for negotiating your salary: adopt a negotiating mindset, know your worth, and think total compensation.

1. Adopt a Negotiation Mindset

Negotiating a salary is the new norm and very commonplace. The best employers expect you to negotiate. They are prepared for it, meaning their first offer is not likely their best. You're most successful when your bargaining power is greatest—at the time of an offer. An offer means you are their candidate of choice. They want you to say yes; they want you motivated and engaged from day one. However, people receiving a job offer often think to themselves, *"I'm unemployed / not happily employed, and need a job. If I try to negotiate, they might rescind their offer."*

They rationalize that the offer on the table may not be ideal, but they think they have no choice or leverage and just want to say yes and end the job search now. The truth is, many don't know their own value and sell themselves short. They don't understand or appreciate what qualities they're actually bringing to the organization. They will often underspeak their talents by being overly modest and failing to say enough about themselves. Whatever your reasons, set that thinking aside. Negotiating is a great way to make a first impression. It indicates that you believe in yourself and your value.

2. Know Your Worth

Setting fear or discomfort with negotiating aside, in most all of our salary negotiation involvements and experience, it always comes down to people not understanding their own worth: the value of their talent, skills, and experience. Why you should negotiate has everything to do with your belief in your value as a person.

Know and believe the value that you place on yourself and the work that you do and be willing to present and defend that value. Begin by determining the external market value of your target role in your particular region of the country. Given that salary range, what is your minimum acceptable number? Keep in mind that if you start from a higher minimum number, you will appear more confident and give yourself more leverage.

There are a number of online salary data sources such as www.salary.com, www.bls.gov, www.glassdoor.com, and www.indeed.com that can help you determine the market value of your position with your experience level. There are also professional and trade organizations that will often post salaries and experience requirements for those positions.

There are also your networks. Chapter 8 shares the many ways networking can be the best source for information that can not only strengthen your job search, but also help you understand the salaries, pay ranges, and responsibilities of the position in the same or similar industries.

3. Think Total Compensation

When evaluating how much a job pays, most people focus solely on the base salary. However, limiting your attention to your bi-weekly or monthly take-home pay can limit your chances of receiving a fair and broader offer. There are many costs associated with accepting a job offer, especially if it requires moving to another city or state, and most especially if you're uprooting your family.

A secret to successful salary negotiation is to not approach it as a salary negotiation. Think more along the lines of "total" compensation. Base salary is often the most important consideration, but there are other components of a job offer that need to be factored into the equation.

Total compensation is the sum of all your take-home earnings including bonus pay. You may also be eligible for other forms of compensation beyond those numbers. The organization may offer short-term and long-term incentives that may go announced unless asked for. You might also discover other incentives and negotiable factors through your networking connections that aren't offered but the hiring company may consider. Here are the major components of a total compensation package.

Standard Total Compensation Package

Base salary	Vacation
401 (K)	Relocation expenses
Bonus pay	Salary increases timing
Tuition assistance	Professional memberships
Incentive pay percentage	Healthcare insurance
Flex hours	Severance package
Commissions	Retirement plan
Equipment: car, phone, laptop, etc.	Stock options

You can negotiate almost anything nowadays including vacation time, maternity leave, paternity leave, temporary housing, or college tuition. Understanding these components can be tricky but knowing your total compensation, applying discipline in ranking what matters most to you using our Offer Evaluation Form, and knowing what items to negotiate and to what degree using our Negotiation Strategy Grid will help ensure you get the job offer you deserve.

How to Acknowledge a Job Offer
Job offers are most often made verbally, typically over the phone, and your immediate response should always be one of appreciation. Whether you believe the offer is great or not, don't reveal any emotion such as disap-

pointment or elation or attempt to negotiate any items, including salary, until you've had time to analyze thoroughly the entire offer. Your goal at this point is to acknowledge the offer with interest and positivity. You can do that with three brief sentences:

1. Express your gratitude: *"Thank you so much for the offer."*

2. Express your interest in joining the team/organization while reinforcing their choice: *"I'm very happy to hear that you've decided I'm the right person for this job and that you want me to join your team."*

3. Buy time: *"When would you like me to get back to you with my response?"*

If you want to confirm what the offer is for or have general questions about unclear details or missing information such as the salary, sign-on bonuses, job responsibilities, benefits, or start date, be direct and speak with confidence. *"Thank you for the offer! I'm delighted to receive your call! The team really impressed me during my last visit! So let me just clarify: the position is_____ and these are the things you want me to accomplish: _____. The salary is _____ and benefits include_____. I want to make a good long-term decision. Can you send me an email with all the details, including benefits? And if it works for you, we can then schedule a time to discuss the offer."*

Avoid, ignore, or downplay ultimatums of any kind in your need to respond to the offer immediately. If a company says, *"I need a response by Monday,"* your response on Monday can be, *"Hello, thank you very much for your offer. I've taken some time to evaluate it and I have a number of questions. I'd like to set up some time with you tomorrow afternoon or the following day to talk through these items."*

Evaluating an Offer

In our practice, we always recommend to those in the process of seeking a job or career change and are beginning to receive offers to ask the employer to share their negotiation strategy and what's open for negotiation. This is especially critical for someone seeking an executive-level position. You could do so by asking, *"Please explain to me the negotiation style of your organization so that I don't offend anyone."*

If a company representative actually says that this is our first and final offer, then that means it's really their first and final offer. There is still opportunity for you to negotiate, however, by asking if there are other elements in the compensation package that can be discussed. You may be fine with the base salary, but there may be other things that you want taken into account such as daycare, transportation, or temporary housing. Your new job may be in an office park further from your home and there will be far more wear and tear on your vehicle.

There are many things to take into account and you should be prepared for the offer or offers that you'll receive. For that task, we have developed an Offer Evaluation Form that categorizes over 70 factors that may be considered when presented with a job offer. Since priorities are different among individuals, this form helps you define which factors are most important to you by using a ranking system that helps you prioritize which factors are your "must haves," your "obtain if possible," and your "nice frills." You can then compare opportunities.

This is a valuable decision-making aid that is made even more powerful through your research. Here is the topline of the evaluation form. You can find the entire form with all 70 factors in Appendix A at the end of this chapter.

Before you receive an offer, begin working on the "Ideal" and "Previous" columns first. Apply values to each of the factors in the six areas of focus from the perspective of your ideal job and your previous positions to determine which elements are most important to you. There are 70 factors distributed among these six areas of focus though not all may apply to your situation. If a factor is irrelevant leave it blank.

Notice that the first two areas of focus are the company and the role you're applying for before attention is given to compensation. If your intent

Offer Evaluation Form

Areas of Focus	Rank	Ideal	Previous	Company A Option A		Company B Option B	
				Terms	Rate	Terms	Rate
Company							
Job							
Compensation							
Relocation							
Personal							
Community							

is to career with purpose, it has to be the right role and the right company first. This parallels the *Career Hierarchy of Needs* pyramid that we shared in Chapter 9.

Once you know your purpose, your next needs are to be engaged in work that allows you to grow within that purpose and to be in a company and culture that shares your values. If you believe those needs are satisfied, then you can shift your attention to compensation and the other three areas of focus. Here is a brief description of the contents of each area:

- Company Focus includes such factors as products or services, financial condition, size, and company culture. Do you believe in their products and services? Are they a stable company? Are they vulnerable to takeovers?

- Job Focus includes elements such as responsibilities, challenge, authority, reporting relationships, travel, title, and admin support.

- Compensation Focus includes such factors as salary, bonuses, profit-sharing, medical plan, vacation, sick leave, home office expenses, car, computer, and cell phone.

- Relocation Focus delineates items such as moving expenses, temporary living costs, per-diem expenses, and closing costs.

- Personal Focus centers on factors such as the job's alignment with your career purpose, promotion potential, company culture, management style, and hybrid work options.

- Community Focus includes location, public transportation, schools, daycare, cultural activities, and recreation.

The next step is to use the Rank column to rate each job factor according to your interest and priority. Rank only those factors that are important to you. A simple rating system of A, B, and C can be used to prioritize factors where A is very important and C is least important. Next is to rank your A's, B's, and C's as A1, A2, A3, and so on.

The Option columns are for actual and likely job offers you want to assess. We use a rating system of 1 through 5, where 1 means "below requirements" and 5 means "exceeds requirements." By using this system, you can compare each offer to your previous and ideal positions as well as against other offers.

The Offer Evaluation Form helps you identify the job factors you may want to negotiate to obtain a closer fit to your ideal position, and ultimately helps you decide which position to accept. You may want to use a high-lighter to accentuate those rows with your highest ranked, or "A" factors. This provides an at-a-glance perspective that takes your eyes directly to those elements most important to you.

Know Your Walk-Aways

The key to any negotiation is knowing your Walk-Away Points. Make sure that you understand the full cost of everything they're offering you. As example, what is the cost of your portion of the employer's group health insurance plan? Currently, it is 17 percent for self-only premiums and as high as 27 percent for family premiums.

According to the Kaiser Family Foundation, in 2021, the average cost of employee health insurance premiums for family coverage was $22,221. The average annual premium for a self-only plan was $7,739. [39] Also take into account that health care costs are climbing at almost twice the rate of annual cost of living salary adjustments. You may want $150k a year, but you and your family can live off of $110K if the company is taking care of 100 percent of your healthcare benefits, giving you a car, and paying for all maintenance on the vehicle.

There's a lot to consider when assessing an offer. We coach our clients to be strategic in their thinking and utilize a strategy grid to assess an offer and establish parameters for what you will and will not accept.

Negotiating Strategy Grid

Offer Item	Offer	Proposal (Target)	Rationale	Option(s)	Walk-Away Point
Salary	$70k	$80k	Market value / Abilities	Accelerate merit raise review	$75k
Vacation	2 weeks	4 weeks	Years of experience above job description requirements	Flex time / comp time	3 weeks
Medical	30-day wait	No wait	$2k out of pocket in COBRA	$2k sign-on bonus grossed up 30% for taxes	Offer as is
Bonus	None	25%	Market research shows positions at this level tend to have bonuses	Ask to re-value position to one that is bonus eligible	Offer as is
Relocation	$20k	$50K (moving co. / house-hunting trip / 30-day housing & expenses / closing costs, etc.)	Estimates from moving cos. / plane fare & hotel / temp living costs while selling home / travel back and forth	Sign-on bonus / corp. housing, telecommuting until house sells	$20K plus temporary housing costs

As you can see, it's more than just title and salary that comprise a job offer. Using this Negotiation Strategy Grid will help you think through and put into perspective all of the monetary values of the offer presented to you and arrive at a package that meets your needs and expectations.

Negotiating the Offer

Once you receive an offer, always request an in-person meeting if possible to review and negotiate the offer or a video conference call if distance is an issue. Never send an email or letter explaining your position. Strive to have a conversation over the subject, then follow up with a detailed email on the points discussed or request of them an email or letter reflecting any negotiated changes.

Project a positive, enthusiastic, relaxed, and conversational tone throughout the meeting. At the onset, restate your comments made when the initial offer was received by saying, *"Thank you so much for the offer. I'm very happy to hear that you've decided I'm the right person for this job and you want me to join your team. I do have a few questions for you."*

Mention points of agreement, but also indicate you have several areas for discussion. *"The benefit package looks great, but I do have a few things that I'd like to discuss."*

Present all of your "asks" at once. Don't surprise them with additional requests later in the meeting. Start with the non-salary items first such as relocation expenses, sign-on bonus, profit-sharing, or home office expenses. Be prepared to share your reasons for each request. Respond positively after each answer where possible to build an expectation that the gap to your accepting a negotiated offer is continually closing. Reaffirm points of agreement related to offer specifics. *"Thank you. That all sounds very good and covers all my general questions. There is one more item."*

Present your salary "ask" once all non-salary items are agreed to and, most important, be specific and prepared to rationalize your request. *"Based on my research, the base salary offered is below the current market rate for similar roles and individuals with my skills and experience."*

Remind the employer what *they* said about your value. *"Also, in our conversations during the interview process, you commented several times about the added value I would bring to the role due to my experience with _____, _____ and _____. How can we close this gap?"*

The ball is now in their court. Stay silent and wait for a response. Their answer may come in the form of a question such as, *"Do you have a specific number in mind?"* or *"What do you think would be a more appropriate salary offer?"*

Be prepared to present your specific counteroffer. *"Based on my research and what I bring to the role, I'm looking for a base salary of $_____. Of course, I'm looking for a positive outcome and I'm confident that we can work through this item successfully."*

The key negotiation is to state clearly your position and be silent. It may feel uncomfortable but it's a valuable tactic. Companies' attorneys and HR managers are trained and skilled at waiting silently. Silence can be deafening, but don't get eager to fill in the quietness with chatter. Waiting it out indicates your conviction and gives them the latitude and the room to think.

If the employer can't give you an immediate response and pledges to get back to you, reiterate your delight at having received the offer and remind them you look forward to joining the team. Graciously thank them for their time and consideration and state that you hope to hear from them soon. Leave them knowing that you believe a mutually beneficial outcome can be reached.

What to Do If They Refuse

As we shared at the onset of this chapter, the odds are clearly in your favor when you negotiate your job offer. However, if you find in the company's response to your counteroffer that you don't get everything you're looking for, stay at the table. It's acceptable to negotiate a second time. Remain positive. Remember, they want you. They expect you to negotiate and the way that you do it with sound reasoning and enthusiasm reflects even more on how you'll handle rejection and continue to negotiate on their behalf.

Don't be afraid to counter but know when to stop or walk away. Help them understand why you deserve what you're requesting. Speak to how you'd be valuable to the company and be specific. *"I understand where you're coming from, and I just want to reiterate my enthusiasm for the position and working with you and the team. I think my skills are perfectly suited for this position and are worth $65,000."*

If they don't accept your counteroffer, recall what we said at the onset: it's not just about salary but total compensation. If your other "asks" have been fulfilled you may decide to accept the role and take the next step in your career knowing that you achieved the best compensation for yourself. They will also know that they are dealing with an authentic person who knows their worth and is willing to fight for it.

Closing the Deal

Once an acceptable solution has been agreed upon, both sides should thank each other for the discussion, no matter the outcome of the negotiation. Successful negotiations are all about creating and maintaining good long-term relationships. At the end of the session, express positive feelings about the agreement you've reached. Ask to have the details of what you've agreed upon—salary and non-salary items—put in writing, but also be prepared to make your own notes during the meeting of what was agreed to.

How you end your negotiation will have everything to do with your ability to reopen that conversation in the future. Show your enthusiasm and appreciation for their taking the time to have the conversation with you, and then reaffirm, *"I'm so excited to be able to work here. I'm looking forward to being a part of your company!"*

Closing the Search

Closing the deal with an organization and accepting their offer is the first step in closing this chapter in your career. Closing the search is the next step and actually the beginning of the next chapter of your work life. Your intent in closing the search is to inform all those you interacted with during your job or career search process that you have accepted a position that you are excited about and are moving forward with your new employer.

Begin by contacting the organizations that you interviewed with that haven't yet made an offer. Express your appreciation for the time they've given you and your admiration for their company and culture. If you were interviewed by a panel, send a letter to each of the interviewers thanking them for their time and letting them know of your decision.

Show confidence by communicating, *"I just wanted to thank you for all the time and energy you spent with me getting to know who I am, but I've accepted an offer at Company ABC and am very happy with my role there now."*

Consider also contacting the organizations that didn't make you an offer saying, *"Thank you for the time that you spent with me. Although I didn't get the job with your organization, I did take a job with Company ABC. I just want to thank you for your interest in me and for giving me an opportunity to speak with you."*

Recall in Chapter 8, we shared the need for building and maintaining your professional network. To that end, it's very important to keep all these new connections alive—even while you're employed—so they know where you are and what you're doing. Your openness and willingness to share where you've landed also brings your personal brand to life through your confident tone and optimism. It also enables others to learn more about who you are and what you represent.

Questions to Reflect On

1. Thinking back to the job offers you've received over the course of your career, which of those could you have negotiated better on your behalf?

2. How do you determine your worth: the value of your talent, skills, and experience? What reasoning do you use to justify what you're requesting in salary and total compensation?

3. What additional ground rule to effective negotiating would you add to our list of adopting a negotiation mindset, knowing your worth, and thinking total compensation?

4. Company and Job come before Compensation in the six areas of focus on our Job Evaluation Form. How would you order the six areas?

5. What would you include in your definition of total compensation? What personal or community asks would you want an employer to agree to in order to make the offer acceptable?

6. When you review a job offer, what would you consider your non-negotiables? What are your walk-away points?

Appendix A: Offer Evaluation Form

Areas of Focus	Rank	Ideal	Previous	Company A / Option A Terms	Rate	Company B / Option B Terms	Rate
Company							
Size of company							
Sales volume							
No. of employees							
Public/Private							
Profit/Non-Profit							
National / Multinational							
Academic							
Product/Service							
Centralized / Decentralized							
Division / Subdivision							
Mgt. depth							
Financial condition							
Political climate							
Growth history							
Profitability							
Future growth							
Turnaround Options							
Stability							

Areas of Focus	Rank	Ideal	Previous	Company A		Company B	
				Option A		Option B	
				Terms	Rate	Terms	Rate
Company (*cont'd*)							
Vulnerability to takeovers							
Reputation							
Market dependence							
Company Culture							

Areas of Focus	Rank	Ideal	Previous	Company A		Company B	
				Option A		Option B	
				Terms	Rate	Terms	Rate
Job Focus							
Business / Position objectives							
Duties / Responsibilities							
Authority							
Independence							
Challenge							
High / Low risk							
Job visibility							

Areas of Focus	Rank	Ideal	Previous	Company A Option A		Company B Option B	
				Terms	Rate	Terms	Rate
Job Focus *cont'd*							
Reporting Relationships							
Travel							
Status (title)							
Admin Assistant							
History / Previous incumbent							
Other:							

Areas of Focus	Rank	Ideal	Previous	Company A Option A		Company B Option B	
				Terms	Rate	Terms	Rate
Compensation							
Base salary							
Bonus (guaranteed)							
Bonus (potential)							
Profit sharing / Gain sharing							
Stock options							

Areas of Focus	Rank	Ideal	Previous	Company A Option A		Company B Option B	
				Terms	Rate	Terms	Rate
Compensation *cont'd*							
Performance evals / merit raise							
Deferred comp							
Benefits – basic health							
Major medical							
Wellness benefits							
Life insurance							
Disability / STD-LTD							
Home office expenses							
Compensation *(cont'd)*							
Retirement / Pension plan							
Addition vacation							
Sick time / PTO							
Car / Car allowance							
Parking							
Club / Association membership							
Credit card(s)							

Areas of Focus	Rank	Ideal	Previous	Company A Option A Terms	Rate	Company B Option B Terms	Rate
Compensation *cont'd*							
Financial Planning							
Tax assistance							
Expense account							
Professional dues							
Tuition assistance							
Cell phone							
Laptop							
Smartphone / Tablet							
Airline VIP Club(s)							
Spouse travel							
Election to board							
(Exec.) Committee(s)							
Other:							

Areas of Focus	Rank	Ideal	Previous	Company A		Company B	
				Option A		Option B	
				Terms	Rate	Terms	Rate
Relocation							
Moving expenses							
Temporary living costs							
Mortgage differential							
Moving insurance							
Per diem costs							
Closing costs							
Severance package							
Outplacement assistance							
Other:							

Areas of Focus	Rank	Ideal	Previous	Company A			Company B	
				Option A			Option B	
				Terms		Rate	Terms	Rate
Personal Focus								
Interpersonal chemistry								
Management style								
Step in career path								
Promotional potential								
Work hours								
commute								
Compatibility with lifestyle								
Other:								

Areas of Focus	Rank	Ideal	Previous	Company A Option A		Company B Option B	
				Terms	Rate	Terms	Rate
Community							
Location / Relocation							
Public transportation							
City / Country Living							
Schools							
Daycare							
Religious affiliation							
Cultural activities							
Recreational areas							
Local taxes							
Other:							

11

Being Present in Your New Role

"The only thing that is real about your journey is
the step that you are taking at this moment."
—Eckhart Tolle

We have shared a great deal with you over the course of our journey on why and how to career with purpose. Yet, it is what you have accomplished thus far that is most meaningful. You have unearthed your authentic story, found your purpose, and made it your brand. You have built an inner circle of support around you and you have interviewed well.

Now, you've been made an offer, which you've accepted, and your new job has meaning for you. What do you do next to make this move the best move of your career? This chapter is about how to onboard with purpose, be the brand that is authentically you, become an integral part of your new organization, and acquire a new heading on your personal long-term career goals.

Job and career transitions can be a difficult time for people. Moving into a new role in a new company is one of the biggest challenges you can face in your work life. While transitions offer a chance to start fresh and make needed changes, there's a lot of uncertainty that comes with a new job. You'll encounter new people, a new culture and way of doing things, and a new set of responsibilities. To help ensure your success, this chapter provides the principles and methods you can use to help guide you through your first milestone months and stay true to your path.

Transitioning with Purpose

Our book has been all about bringing purpose and committed effort to everything involving your career. This includes how you manage your transition into your new organization. We have concentrated that undertaking down to these six practices:

1. **Prepare Yourself.** Be deliberate about defining who you want to be and what you want to be known for.

2. **Learn the Organization.** You may be the best at what you do, but *prioritize listening and learning first* before recommending or enacting change. Seek to understand the history and legacy of decisions. Understand the why.

3. **Have Personal Objectives.** Develop the goals that you want to achieve and map out how you plan to accomplish them in your first 90 days.

4. **Build Relationships.** Be curious about others. Show that you genuinely want to get to know them by listening and asking questions.

5. **Accelerate Your Learning.** Know what skills gaps you want to close and find opportunities that will allow you to gain that knowledge and experience.

6. **Secure Early Wins.** Be judicious about the initial projects you take on. Pace yourself to build followership and create momentum.

To get to this point, you successfully navigated the most challenging parts of the hiring process. Now, the real work begins. Your next step is to focus on your first three months and to map the new path of your career from your current position. It is all about building relationships now, learning about the company and its culture, and becoming an essential part of the organization. Let's look more deeply into the six personal undertakings that we consider essential to your success.

1. Prepare Yourself

Your first task is to take a moment and reflect on the unfolding of your career. You've chosen to leave a job or renew your current brand at your organization, or you've decided to pursue an entirely new career. We all get to choose what we do for a living and you've made your choices. Preparing yourself is being very deliberate before starting your new job about defining who you want to be, what you want your legacy to be, and how you intend to achieve your goals.

Be genuine in showing integrity and accountability in the persona you project. Be the person who takes responsibility for your actions by demonstrating your reliability and trustworthiness. In *Leadership ON PURPOSE,* Grubich and Smith shared the importance of personal integrity and the shadows cast by leaders that have a huge impact on whether people will trust and follow them.[40]

Whether a leader or an individual contributor, we all have a shadow that we cast that is both ahead of us and behind us and is either positive or negative in its projection. What do you want your shadow saying about you before you enter a room and after you leave? Ask yourself this and other related questions to help you articulate your intentions and sharpen your resolve.

- *What do I want to be known for?* What kind of person do I want to be, not so much by my words but more so by my conduct and actions? What do I want my legacy to be?

- *How will I hold myself accountable?* What actions will I take to ensure that I'm being the person that I want to be?

- *What mistakes do I want to avoid?* What have I learned from my past experiences that I'll modify and approach differently now?

- *What successful outcomes do I want to replicate?* Which of my past experiences were successful and why? What measures could I take in my new role to pave the way for future successes?

- *How will I balance my work and personal life?* Given this new position, what changes will come to my personal life and that of my family? What are my plans to maintain harmony between those two worlds?

All of us are aiming for something greater in our work life. You can achieve things above and beyond what you thought possible if you know what's driving you and what gets you out of bed every day. Having control over your career requires you to be intentional. Purposeful, mindful actions yield better results and can lead to better projects, quicker promotions, and higher salaries. By knowing your purpose and using it to guide you, you can become far more productive and resilient and find personal satisfaction and happiness in your work.

2. Learn the Organization

This practice is about learning the history of your organization. Where and how did it get its start, what momentum gave it its growth, and what forces are sustaining it today? Learning the organization is knowing its purpose and values, what the plaques represent on the walls, and what the unwritten rules, procedures, and policies are.

You may be the best at what you do, but learning how the organization works, not just what it makes, is critically important for your success in your first 90 days. You may be the best violinist in the world, but if you don't listen for and learn the pace and volume of the other orchestra members, you'll never blend in and know where and when to heighten your sound. Regrettably, it's a common motivation for new leaders and managers feeling the need to make their mark to do just the opposite by drowning out everyone else and driving into change head first.

John went to West Point, one of the top educational institutions in the United States, and received a great education in computer science. Over the next ten years, he worked at three different companies where he established a powerful track record for designing award-winning software programs.

John recently accepted an offer from an innovative tech company wanting to grow their Enterprise Resource Planning services. This was a great opportunity for John, but just as with the other three companies, John came in with the single intent of revamping each company's software development processes. History was repeating itself for John, for just as with his last positions with each ending in his leaving, he didn't take the time to learn the company and its processes and procedures, and equally important, build relationships and followership.

It's quite possible that, given his experience and expertise, John's approach and recommended changes may have been better, perhaps even far better. However, that's not what was important for John to prove first. He first needed to demonstrate his intentions to learn and respect the organization and its people. New executives face intense pressure to produce positive results quickly, and they often make unilateral decisions without truly understanding the potential impact those changes can have on their companies, their teammates, or themselves.

John went in with a hammer looking for nails to pound. With that mindset, it doesn't matter what he sees because he'll always see nails, and he'll try to hit those nail heads as hard as he can because he believes that's the person he needs to be.

You need to prioritize listening and learning. One of the top reasons executives fail is because they try to effect change too quickly to prove their worth to others or possibly even to themselves. Take that tack and you'll eventually lose allies and offend co-workers because you didn't take the time to recognize and respect them and their work.

As the new employee, people are going to be judging you, watching you, and looking for your strengths and weaknesses. They're going to call out your mistakes quicker. If you're an outsider in a role for which there were internal candidates for promotion, they're not going to be supporting you one hundred percent out of the gate. You have to first prove yourself by learning and respecting the organization and its people, then easing into your objectives.

3. Have Personal Objectives

In addition to the responsibilities and objectives that come with the position, strive to have your own objectives. Spend time reflecting on those things that you want to accomplish in your new role and map out exactly how you plan to accomplish them in a 30-, 60-, and 90-day timeframe. Reaffirm also what your long-term objectives are for your career. Just as intentional as you were in your process for finding a new job, you want your engagement with your new organization to be just as purposeful and strategic.

In Chapter 7, we wrote of our coaching people in the process of outplacement to "go slow to go fast" and bring more mindfulness into their next career move. We have found time and again that the preparations that you make in the first two weeks of your job search will have a profound impact on the duration of time you're unemployed. In the same vein, the preparations that you make in the initial weeks and months in your new role can have an equally profound impact on the extent of your success in your new role.

The 30-, 60-, and 90-day planning section further on in this chapter is intended to help you think through your objectives, define your priorities, and measure your success. Once you know what your goals are for your new role and for yourself, your next associated step is to find a way to keep yourself true to your path and responsible for your performance.

Hold Yourself Accountable

As you define and plan out the attainment of your goals, what are your plans to hold yourself accountable to the steps you laid out for yourself in the pursuit of your objectives? One approach is to have someone else hold you answerable for your actions and behaviors. Your immediate supervisor is an obvious first choice since many of your objectives will be tied to the expectations of your role. Have conversations with your manager to review your plans and to check in with you at milestone intervals to help keep you on track. In addition to your manager supporting and encouraging you, a career mentor can be a valuable person in your corner.

Unfortunately, the contribution of career mentors is so vastly underrated and so often misapplied. As example, many seek career mentors for the sole (and we believe short-sighted) reason of finding help and advice in advancing their careers. The correct approach is to first plan out what you want to do with your work life, then seek a career mentor or someone in your inner circle whom you can trust to hold you accountable to the person you want to be and to the legacy you intend on building for yourself.

In the appendix at the end of this chapter, you'll find <u>Insights to Action</u>, a personal diary that allows you to check in with yourself and help hold you accountable to your 30-, 60-, 90-day plan by encouraging you to journal at each monthly interval your challenges, feelings, concerns, successes, and mistakes.

4. Build Relationships

Building positive relationships with co-workers is important for your career. All data show that people who have positive relationships with one another are more likely to perform well when working together on a project. Having teammates whom you respect can motivate you as well to perform to the best of your abilities. Collaborative relationships can also help transfer skills between more experienced workers and those with less experience.

We believe the best way to build relationships quickly is to be as curious about others and their work as they are of you as the new person. Understand their roles and how you can be of value to them, and in turn how they may be of value to you. Acknowledging your co-workers' presence and value and empathizing with them will immediately start the relationship-building process, for your showing genuine interest alone will leave them feeling positive about you being on their team.

Prepare a brief introduction of yourself ahead of time so you have a script in mind when you encounter someone new. Show conviction, positivity, and optimism each time you talk about yourself, your accomplishments, and your interests. Introduce yourself frequently but be aware of your surroundings. Don't interrupt people to introduce yourself, and always be brief. As you're speaking, be cognizant of how the other person is reacting. If they seem receptive, make an effort to get to know that individual better. Show that you genuinely want to meet them and get to know who they are by listening and asking questions.

It's very important to remember names and the best way to remember is by paying extra attention. Attention is the foundation of memory. Repeat the person's name more than once while speaking with them. If they have a complicated name, ask them to spell it. Connect the name and face to someone or something familiar. And always use the person's name at the end of the conversation. Once the conversation is over, make a quick note about them and their interests. If you forget someone's name the next time you see them, be honest by saying, *"My apologies, I've been taking in a lot of new information over the last few days. Please remind me of your name?"*

5. Accelerate Your Learning

Train with purpose. Think analytically about the knowledge gaps that will exist for you as the new person on the block. Which of your skills will easily transfer to the new role, and what skills will need to be learned or relearned? Understanding what you know and what you don't know is precisely where your own learning plan begins. Also ensure that what you are learning aligns with your career goals and not just in the service of satisfying the requirements of your current position.

If you plan properly, you should be able to identify those things that you need to learn and when. Know what gaps you want to close in your own skillset, and with your manager's support, seek out opportunities in your organization that will allow you to achieve that knowledge and experience. Building good relationships, particularly with senior employees, can help accelerate your learning.

An important part of accelerating your learning is to practice Habit #5 of Stephen Covey's *The 7 Habits of Highly Effective People*: seek first to understand then to be understood.[41] In order to build deep relationships, you need to first truly understand what people are both saying and feeling when in conversation with you. This is all about curiosity and becoming an unbiased sponge intent on absorbing the environment around you.

6. Secure Early Wins

According to Michael Watkins, author of *The First 90 Days*, the best way to get noticed by others is to secure "early wins."[42] This will prop up your credibility and provide an opportunity to invest in key relationships that will be essential for your successful transition into your new role.

As a new employee, manager, or leader, you'll be under a microscope in your first 90 days as your superiors and teammates strive to figure out who you are and what you'll contribute. In the first few weeks, identify opportunities to build personal credibility and make striving to achieve those opportunities a part of your own onboarding plan. However, be careful that you don't create a persona of yourself that isn't sustainable.

I remember when I, Mike Grubich, started my job at Kohler Company as the global director of talent and leadership development. It was early October and my wife, children, and I were fortunate to find a house that we would be able to move into by the end of December. As you may have faced at one time or another in your own life, our challenge was still having to sell our current home.

I rented an apartment near Kohler headquarters for those first two months and then moved into our unfurnished new home in December for an additional two months as we waited for our place to sell. Although I was able to drive home on the weekends, not having my family around during the weekdays left me with a lot of time to fill. I would rise early in the morning to work out, then go into the office and work until late in the evening. I was staying later than everyone else in order to get acclimated and accomplish as much as I could in my first 90 days.

I'll never forget what Laura Kohler, Head of Human Resources at the time, said to me about a month and a half into the job. It was late one evening and Ms. Kohler stopped at my office door and offered this sage advice: *"Mike, you're doing amazing work, but be careful because you're getting so much done. People are going to start to expect that from you. When your family eventually joins you, you're never going to be able to keep up that speed. Pace yourself."*

Her phrase "pace yourself" took on special meaning for me that evening and has guided my efforts ever since. You have to pace yourself if you want to become an integral part of the organization. You certainly want to have quick wins, but be careful not to make running at 140 percent your characteristic way of doing things. People will grow to expect that level of activity from you and you may even grow to expect it of yourself. That will certainly defeat your purpose in finding greater work-life harmony. Prepare yourself to run a marathon, not a sprint. Pace yourself in a way that mirrors the culture and wisely choose your early wins.

Action Priority Matrix

One valuable decision-making tool that can help you learn the rhythm of the organization and assess where to focus your efforts is the Action Priority Matrix. This 2x2 diagram will help you determine which tasks to focus on and in which order. The concept of the matrix was first inspired by Stephen Covey in *The 7 Habits of Highly Effective People*. Covey describes "four quadrants" for dividing tasks based on the tasks you'll do first, the tasks you'll schedule for later, the tasks you'll delegate, and the tasks you'll delete.[43]

Action Priority Matrix

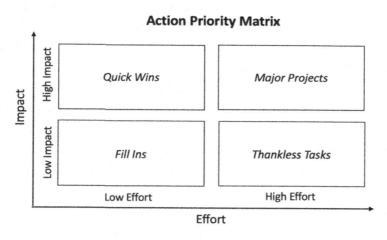

Create your matrix by beginning with two components: "effort" along the x-axis and "impact" along the y-axis. Next, add four boxes or quadrants to plot all of your initiatives by assessing the effort each task will take and the impact each will have: quick wins (high impact, low effort); major projects (high impact, high effort); fill-ins (low impact, low effort); and thankless tasks (low impact, high effort).

Quick wins can gain you the support you'll need for your major projects—tasks that will take more time and most likely require the effort of others. Learn and feel the pace of the organization, emulate that rhythm, and use its momentum to help you achieve what you want to achieve. Making your contribution with a softer, more mindful hand is the best way to influence others and gain followers.

Build Followership

For any project or organization to succeed, there must be people who willingly and effectively follow, just as there must be those who willingly and effectively lead. Followership is your ability to inspire others through your actions and behaviors, to build relationships, and to establish your credibility with others so they can confidently place their faith in you.

It takes humility to admit when you don't know something and be willing to step aside and let someone else take the lead when it's appropriate. It doesn't mean you're less of a leader. You taking a step back means that you're letting someone with greater expertise take the lead. That act in itself of letting others shine will encourage those people, and those watching, to have even greater faith in you.

Consider also that followership is not just the action of someone in a subordinate role. It's also an attribute that complements one's leadership. A confident leader sees the value in seeking out and listening to the insights of others. Ask yourself: how good are you at finding those people inside the organization that you believe can be trusted advisors who can help inspire you?

Your First Days

The first few days in a new job and new organization can give even CEOs the jitters. You don't have to impress and influence all your teammates or implement all your actions on your first day. Just be a sponge, intent on soaking everything up. That's your very first task.

Be prepared to introduce yourself and have your elevator pitch well-rehearsed. Smile and show enthusiasm each time you speak about yourself. Research the office attire at your new place or similar places of work and then look and play the role. Don't dress unprofessionally. Always err on the side of overdressing. It shows your respect for the organization and its people. To that end, don't ignore orientation or any onboarding support that's offered to you. These planned activities will give you a chance to learn more about the organization and its policies and procedures.

Don't be antisocial. If you tend to be introverted, challenge yourself a little to be more open and let people get to know you. Small things such as accepting lunch invitations are so important in these early days. While having lunch, never complain or speak ill about your former company, manager, or co-workers. Stay clear of politics. Be neutral and optimistic. Most important, listen more than talk and be humble and brief when you do. Humility opens the door to meaningful relationships and opportunities to learn.

Mapping Your 30-, 60-, 90-Day Plan

Research and conventional wisdom both suggest that employees get about 90 days to prove themselves in a new job. Surveys **also show that only 12 percent of employees believe that their organization does a great job onboarding new people.**[44]

This means that there's a lot of room for improvement on the part of organizations. What this also means is that *you* have to take the reins for those first 90 days to ensure that you're being disciplined and purposeful as you learn the organization, build valuable relationships, and prioritize your efforts to secure early wins.

While there is no set length for a 30-, 60-, 90-day plan, it should include the goals that you are expected to achieve in your role, along with metrics for each time span. There are many templates that you can find online to help you structure and follow your milestone plan, or you can create your own template. Make certain that each 30-day period includes your key focus for that milestone; what you want to accomplish in that timeframe, what your priorities or strategies will be, and how you will measure your success.

In addition to the goals, responsibilities, and metrics assigned to you by your organization, these are our recommendations on what you should personally strive to attain by each milestone. Bottom line, over the course of your first three months, your intent should be to learn the organization, build strong relationships, and be quickly and intelligently effective in your role.

30-Day Focus

The first 30 days is all about learning the organization's processes and procedures. It's about discovering the pace of work and building relationships with your teammates. Your primary goal is to know your role and responsibilities as they relate to performance, development, and ethical behavior. Your intent should also be to learn the purpose of your role, how it aligns with others on your team and how your work aligns with the objectives and strategies of the entire organization.

Many new managers are eager to get into execution mode right out of the gate. That is seldom to your advantage. The first 30 days require patience. Begin to identify opportunities, but take the time to study them as you learn about how the organization works. Concentrate your initial efforts on absorbing and learning as much as possible about the business, the culture, and your teammates.

60-Day Focus

Within 60 days, you should start to demonstrate an understanding of core business operations. You should also be deciding on what early wins you can secure that have the highest impact with the least amount of effort. Show your manager that you are studying the organization for those early wins. Meet with your manager to present what you've discovered and how you can use their support. Make them aware of your desire to begin contributing to the success of your position and the success of your team.

At the end of 60 days, you should have established a positive image for yourself. People should know you as a doer, a team player, and a good listener. You should be able to speak more at meetings, share your ideas freely, contribute to the overall progress of ideas, and help improve the team's functioning. You should also begin to increase your workload and increase your personal output.

90-Day Focus

By the end of 90 days, you should really be feeling at one with the organization. You should have a firm grasp of your role and the work culture around you. Personally, you should be familiar with everyone on your team and all the stakeholders that are related to your business. In these next 30 days, focus on building on what you have learned in the first 60 and work more toward execution and establishing even greater credibility by continuing to garner wins.

By this point, people should begin viewing you as a leader and be comfortable sharing ideas and experiences with you. At this juncture, start looking into taking up projects outside of your role and collaborating more with other teams. Begin communicating more about what you've been doing and what you intend to do. The metaphor that we often use is to make sure that your bull's-eye is on the right tree as you begin building your brand and making it clear what you want to be known for and how you will start moving forward.

The Next 90 and Beyond

The right perspective is to look upon your 90-day plan as really the next 90 days of your entire career. Through that lens, your plan could easily become a 180-day plan, your first-year plan, and from there your trajectory for the next three to five years. Remember, to career with purpose is to follow your North Star and to make continuous adjustments to your compass heading to ensure you're on the right path for yourself and not drawn off course by someone or something else.

A career is an evolutionary experience, not a revolutionary one. Whether you're fresh out of college or the CEO of a powerful conglomerate, you're going to continue to learn and develop. The art is in continuously going back to reevaluate what you've learned and accomplished and confirm your heading from that position forward.

Be proactive by bringing ideas to your manager to create a career path that aligns with your long-term career intentions. However, keep in mind that your career plan is without regard for the organization you're working for. In your pursuit of a career with purpose, make sure that your efforts are closely aligned with what it is that *you* want to accomplish. Have the courage to be honest about that with your manager. Make clear that you intend to bring success to your position and to the organization, but that you also desire for your position to feed into the long-range goals for your career, which may or may not continue in that organization. What matters most is that you are being true to your authentic self.

Questions to Reflect On

1. What do you want your shadow saying about you before you enter a room and after you leave? What do you want to be known for among your teammates and peers?

2. What personal disciplines do you have or intend to develop to ensure that you're prioritizing listening and learning over attempting to challenge others or effect change too quickly?

3. What actions and behaviors do you exhibit to build credibility with others so they feel they can rely on you and place trust in you?

4. What traits or indications do you look for in people inside the organization whom you believe can be trusted advisors and help inspire you?

5. If you used the Action Priority Matrix in this chapter to assess your projects and focus your efforts, how would you go about controlling or eliminating the "thankless tasks" and spending less time on "fill-ins"?

6. Taking the reverse perspective, when you consider your long-term career objective and reflect back incrementally to the medium- and short-term goals you'll need to accomplish first, does your 90-day plan align with your vision and keep you on that path?

Appendix: Insights to Action

(Check in with Yourself)

Insights to Action is all about measuring your progress and holding yourself accountable to your 30-, 60-, 90-day plan. Your intent is to ensure that you're being the person that you want to be doing the right things right in your new role. Use this resource to check in with yourself and diary your challenges, feelings, concerns, successes, and mistakes at each monthly interval.

What challenges are you facing?

30 Days	
60 Days	
90 Days	

What are you feeling?

30 Days	
60 Days	
90 Days	

What has concerned you?

30 Days	
60 Days	
90 Days	

What has gone well?

30 Days	
60 Days	
90 Days	

What would you like to do over?

30 Days	
60 Days	
90 Days	

12

Is Your Ladder on the Right Wall?

"If the ladder is not leaning against the right wall,
every step we take just gets us to the wrong place faster."
—Stephen Covey

There's a certain work life battle that many people allow themselves to get caught up in. For some, it begins their first day on the job, fresh out of college, and continues on throughout their career; a mad dash to be acknowledged by others as a person of importance. Many scramble to advance and compete in climbing their ladders, regardless of what it is they're trying to accomplish. It becomes a constant competitive struggle comparing their lives and accomplishments to others.

However, with all their achievements, many people who come to us seeking new jobs or new careers are disillusioned and feel uninspired. They speak of an emptiness in their work, of something missing in this world that they've created for themselves. Some complain that they're not climbing their ladders fast enough while others blame their company's management or the culture for not accepting them and validating their talents and stills.

They come to us wondering if they should change jobs or change careers and then find what they believe to be the perfect role in the perfect company. They vow to themselves that things are going to be different this time, though nothing really changes. They fall back into the same mindset and pattern of behavior that ends in disappointment, and within two years, they're job searching again. But without personal change, they're destined to find themselves climbing toward the same outcome.

If you've read each chapter of our book, you've experienced a progression starting with you finding your story and continuing on through to onboarding into your new role. Alternatively, you may have read specific chapters given the stage you're at in your job search. In either event, this final chapter is offered as a reality check and calibration of your heading. We'll be revisiting key areas of our book to help you confirm that your ladder is on the right wall and that your climb from here on is mindful, purposeful, and ultimately fulfilling.

In this final chapter, we're going to approach the question of the right ladder being on the right wall from three perspectives: (1) your ladder may be on the right wall but you could be climbing it all wrong; (2) you're on the right wall but you didn't get the job; and (3) you *are* on the wrong wall and perhaps climbing the wrong set steps. We'll explore each of these outcomes offering our closing perspectives and advice. At the end of the chapter, we also provide a <u>Job Search Checklist</u> and final exercise, <u>Insights into Action,</u> to bring energy, focus, and forward momentum into your search.

How Are You Scaling Your Ladder?

You may have found the perfect role in a great company but you onboarded with high, and perhaps unreasonable, expectations. If three to six months have passed and you're feeling dissatisfied and looking for change again, you may be viewing your career through a short-sighted lens, putting near-term gratification ahead of long-term value. Many people don't realize what it truly means to be on the path toward a fulfilling work life.

In this rush for fulfillment, perhaps it's time to return to the question we asked at the onset of our book. What is the purpose of what you're doing for a living? It may be to provide a comfortable life for your family. You may love to travel or to be a stay-at-home mom or dad and want a job that gives you the freedom to work from anywhere and at any time. You may have an altruistic intent and want to work at resolving community or even global issues.

You can't determine if you're climbing the right ladder and if it's on the right wall unless you know what you want out of the one-third of your life you'll spend working. For many people today, a career journey has more to do with self-discovery and self-care than it does mere advancement. It is also possible that you still may not know what you want out of your work life. Sometimes it takes a hard dose of reality to make clear the difference.

Stephanie jumped at the opportunity to work for a high-tech manufac-turer doing practically the same job she was currently doing at her present company but with a 25 percent increase in salary plus a signing bonus. Four months later, she contacted her former company to ask if she could return. She was even willing to accept a lower position. Stephanie discov-ered that the content of the job and her responsibilities were not what she thought they would be, and equally important to her, she missed the man-agement team and the people she worked with.

Culture, Content, Co-worker

Title and compensation are strong magnets. Those attainments have their value, but if that's all you're seeking or allowing yourself to be lured by, be prepared to be frustrated and unsatisfied. When you look back over the course of your career, you may discover that the greater wealth was embed-ded in the culture of the organization, the content of your work, and in your ability to build relationships with co-workers who shared your values.

Paul was a remarkable salesperson and exceptionally good at devel-oping relationships. He started as a project manager in a privately owned company and worked his way up to become CEO. He discovered that he was quite skilled at running the company and attributed his success to his selling skills, building relationships, and being a problem solver for his cli-ents. After only a year, Paul felt completely disconnected from the work he was doing and decided to step down and accept a sales position in another company. Six months into the new job, Paul realized that selling was no longer something he enjoyed doing.

Contemplating changing jobs or careers can often put people in reflec-tive moods as they consider what could have been and what could be if they followed their dreams. Paul had an aspiration in college to become a high school guidance counselor and help young people take their first steps in making lifelong career decisions. That recollection kept replaying in Paul's mind and grew stronger every day. This time though, he listened. He attended night school and in six months earned a degree in counseling and is now a high school guidance counselor and career advisor. Paul is one of the happiest people we've ever worked with. The wheels didn't come into motion for him until he stepped down from the CEO position. It gave him more time to breathe and think through what it was that he really wanted to do for the remainder of his work life.

Why Didn't You Get the Job?

After having gone through the process of searching and interviewing, you may not have gotten the job you wanted, or you keep striking out even though you enjoy the work you do, you're very good at it, and you can see elements in each company that you align with in terms of interests and values. In our experience, the reason or reasons you may be striking out may have little or nothing to do with your skills and experience but rather your likability, the power of your presence, and your capacity to connect through storytelling. With all things being equal in terms of candidate experience and expertise, these factors unfailingly make the difference in deciding whether someone gets hired.

Are You a Likable Person?

You could be the smartest and most accomplished person in the world, but if you're not likable, people are not going to hire you. Likable people are gregarious, positive, and genuinely interested in others. They have the aptitude to make others feel good about themselves, mainly because they're confident in their own capabilities and comfortable in their own skin. They don't pretend to be someone they're not.

We may not want to judge a book by its cover, but studies have shown that when we see a new face, our brains decide whether a person is likable and trustworthy within a tenth of a second. No words even need to be exchanged.[45] It appears that we are hardwired to draw these inferences in a fast, unreflective way and decide very quickly whether a person possesses many of the traits we feel are important, and likability tops the list because it indicates so many things about you.

Given this potential, it makes sense to walk into your interviews and meetings projecting confidence and a genuine interest in others. It will show on your face and in your body language and believe us, hiring managers can spot confidence (or the lack of it) from across the room.

Do You Have the Power of Presence?

Candidates who connect well during job interviews have presence; they look self-assured and relaxed, and they speak clearly and persuasively, even under pressure. The power of presence goes beyond likability and is all about how you show up. It's your energy level and expression and enthusiasm. When you are fully present, you are focused on others rather than yourself.

People with a strong presence are often very charismatic and attract people to them like a magnet. So much of charisma stems from self-confidence. It's being practiced without being rote. It's knowing your value and believing in yourself and what you stand for. It's also knowing what's important to you, that which you will not compromise. Having that mindset and showing up for the interview with that quiet self-assuredness will show itself in your body language without you even having to say a word.

However, when you do speak, do so to convince your audience through your words and stories that you uniquely know how to solve their problem, that you're a thought leader in your profession, and that you are the expert they need to fill the position.

Are You a Good Storyteller?

Storytelling during the interview process is the third in this trio of life skills and can be an Achilles' heel for even the most brilliant minds. The whole point is to be able to portray your value to an organization through an example of something you accomplished; what your approach was and why it was important for you to take that particular tack; how you gained consensus; how you attacked the situation; and what the end result was. The skill is in telling your story in a way that creates an emotional experience for the listener and helps them see you in the role and as a part of their organization.

Elliot, one of those brilliant minds, is a highly successful chief legal counsel for a very large organization in Chicago. He made it to the final round of interviews with three organizations and wasn't accepted for the position of general counsel by any of them. He couldn't understand why. We mock-interviewed with Elliot to see if we could unearth why he was striking out. We found that he was infallible in remembering and reciting legal precedents, yet what he was missing was a passion in his voice beyond the casework that indicated why he wanted to practice law in that organization. He wasn't making that emotional connection in his interviews.

Your presence is a huge part of your brand. It may be everything, because aside from your resume and social media profile, how you show up is all a recruiter, HR professional, or hiring manager may have to go on. For about one-third of the people we work with, not getting the job has everything to do with the stories they're not telling.

It May Not Have Been Your Fault

Your ladder may be on the right wall and you may have executed everything correctly, but you still didn't get the job. It may not have been something you did or failed to do. There may have been highly suitable people vying for the same position as you. Only one-tenth of one percent of college athletes make the pros; and there are many, many skilled young athletes who don't make the cut each year. The same holds true in every single profession. There may be a host of other reasons why someone else was selected over you:

- The hiring manager had a certain type of person in mind for the job, whether for their age, gender, background, education, certifications, etc., and hired someone who matched that profile.

- The candidate they hired was somehow connected to the organization. Perhaps they were a vendor or a customer, or knew someone who worked for the firm.

- Perhaps the successful candidate answered the hiring manager's questions just the way they wanted the questions to be answered.

Maybe you were too out-of-the-box for them. In that case, it may not have been the best organization for your long-term happiness.

- You could have unintentionally threatened the hiring manager with your confidence and competence. This often happens when hiring managers lack the self-confidence to hire someone stronger than themselves.

- It could be that they really wanted to hire you, but the other candidate was willing to do the job for less money.

You may never know why you didn't get the job, and the more it matters to you, the more of your personal power and positivity will drain out of you. In these situations, people will often take a step back to determine what it was they did wrong when in reality they did nothing wrong. You don't have time to waste trying to figure out exactly why people you met with for four or five hours made the decision to hire someone else. You are on the right path. Trust in that. You have to be resilient, accept that that opportunity didn't work out for you, dust yourself off, and pursue other opportunities.

It doesn't necessarily mean you should change your strategy either. It just means that it didn't work out this time. To that end, you should have ladders on as many walls as possible. Practice your storytelling. Learn to better convey your experience, your skills, and your passion so that people can easily understand your value, believe you, and believe in you.

Maybe You *Are* on the Wrong Wall

Are you doing the right things for you? As we shared in the first few pages of our book, at some point in your life, you have to address the stories that you've chosen to believe about who you are, what your career path should be, and what you can and can't do. Have you written your own story, defined your own purpose, and used that discovery and declaration as the bearing for your career?

Are you managing your expectations of yourself? Perhaps you've created an expectation of yourself and your ladder isn't on the best possible wall for you, and now you're feeling disappointed in yourself for not getting the job. Take stock again of the things that you've accomplished in your work life thus far. What roles and activities over the years have you completed exceptionally well? What comes natural to you and brings you the greatest enjoyment and sense of personal satisfaction? Are you leveraging those strengths now?

Are you managing the expectations of others? Others' expectations of you, regardless of how close they are to you, don't take into account your true talents, inclinations, and deepest desires, or what is even possible or realistic for you. Are you centered around what's most important to you?

Are you managing societal expectations? The expectations placed on us by society and the world we live in are the most difficult to contend with and triumph over. For a young person, social pressure comes from all corners of their lives including family, school, friends, social media, movies, and music.

Challenge yourself enough to ask yourself these questions and be courageous and willing to listen to your answers. Why not take that introspective step? Having a lifetime of happiness in what you're doing for a living is well worth the extra effort. It's all about your mindset and the direct bearing it has on your beliefs and on the actions you take.

People get so locked into believing that *"this is what I want to do for a living"* or *"this is what I have to do"* that they miss the signs to job or career opportunities that could be a better fit for them. Yet, they've grown to believe and have convinced themselves, for whatever reason, that the work they engaged in or the career they've chosen is what they want or have to do.

In *Leadership ON PURPOSE,* Grubich and Smith distinguish between growth and fixed mindsets as they pertain to how leaders approach challenges and disruptions.[46] The same classification can be applied to how you view your job and career. A fixed mindset views situations and events as being unchangeable and simply things that can be managed. A growth mindset believes that each situation is nothing more than a starting point, and their role is being present at its beginning to direct the outcome and allow themselves to be directed by it. It's often difficult for us to see and accept ourselves fully. This is when you can use your network to confide in and help you view your situation and your options from different perspectives.

Look Inward, Outward, and Forward

Our Framework for Career Discussions in Chapter 2 is a valuable drill for thinking through your job and career choices and for reading the signs to determine if a change is a good move for you, and in which direction. The three thought exercises of looking inward, outward, and forward that we propose require your honest consideration.

Begin by looking inward. The motivation for reading your own signs has to be there first. Is how you view your talents and capabilities a result of the stories that you've chosen to believe about who you are and what you're capable of doing and achieving? Recognizing and releasing yourself of these constraints takes courage. Assess what you've accomplished and are capable of doing; determine the impact you want to have; then plan out the direction you want your capabilities to carry you.

The next step is to look outward. Research your company, your industry, and the marketplace. How are your company and the organizations you're targeting performing in your industry? Where are the growth trends in your industry and what is the impact technology will have on those trends? Are you connected to a diverse network of business associates who have greater knowledge and experience than you do on trends and on the companies you're pursuing?

The third exercise is looking forward by assessing what you've discovered by looking inward and outward. When you weigh your personal goals and desires against your satisfiers and dissatisfiers, is the company you're with enabling your journey? Is it big enough to allow you the vertical climbing space or lateral moves to whatever job or career you want to pursue?

The S.T.A.R. Model

Many organizations use behavioral interviewing techniques to focus on a candidate's past experiences and assess how they've handled situations in the past and applied skills relevant to the position they're interviewing for. Rather than asking theoretical questions such as, *"How would you handle this situation?,"* interviewers focus instead on concrete experiences by asking, *"How did you handle that situation?"* It's a technique to evaluate your past behavior in order to predict your future actions, and you need to be prepared to answer these types of questions.

We recommend creating brief S.T.A.R. stories prior to the interview that demonstrate your teamwork abilities, highlight your planning and leadership skills, and show your problem-solving skills. Utilizing the S.T.A.R. method will help you construct an organized, thoughtful, and concise answer.

Situation – think of a situation in which you were involved that had a positive outcome.

Task – describe the tasks involved in the situation.

Action – specify what actions you took to complete the tasks and achieve your results.

Results – itemize the results that followed because of your actions.

Be as relevant as possible to the position you're seeking and be prepared to provide examples of occasions when results were different than you expected. Practice your stories, but be careful not to memorize as you may forget nuances of your story when pressured. Reviewing your S.T.A.R. stories before your interview will give you confidence in knowing you are prepared and will eliminate fumbling for words and awkward silences in the interview.

Continuing Your Journey

We've shared a lot of insights, tools, and resources with you in our book on unearthing your story and careering with purpose. We hope you'll refer to this book often and review the questions and exercises you did at the end of each chapter as a reminder of what's important to you and what you want to accomplish in your career.

Stay focused on that vision for yourself and we can assure you that you're going to find something that is right for you. It may take time, but don't compromise your values and resist all urges to change who you are just to land the position. Don't be disappointed if it doesn't always work out for you. It doesn't mean you made the wrong choice; it just means it wasn't the right opportunity for you at that point in time.

As we shared at the onset of our journey, your career is like your North Star. No matter how far you travel, how much time you invest in getting there, or the amount of effort you apply, you'll never arrive at the North Star. Continue on your journey and make adjustments to your compass heading as you encounter different and challenging terrain to ensure you're always on the true path toward your goal. Accept that you will never arrive at being your ideal self; you will never be "finished" as a perfect human being. To that end, continue to assess where you're going, what you've learned, and what impact you want to have in your life and the lives of those you cross paths with as you career with purpose.

Job Search Checklist

An important component of our practice is to create a checklist for the people we work with as it relates to their job or career search. Successfully navigating your transition from one organization to another is a complex process. This list of action items that form the foundation for a job search—from planning your move to onboarding—will help ensure you're comprehensive in your approach. We always recommend having a career discussion with your current employer to explore opportunities before looking elsewhere. To that end, this checklist assumes you've determined that your dissatisfiers outweigh your satisfiers and you are ready to move forward.

Readiness for Moving Forward
- [ ] Reason for leaving statement
- [ ] Closure with current employer
- [ ] Financial/personal/family plan for transition
- [ ] Summary statement for evolved resume and LinkedIn page

Personal Brand Development
- [ ] Relate your story to your digital brand
- [ ] Identify audience by needs and content expectations
- [ ] Communicate with consistency in messaging across mediums
- [ ] Build network of supporters

Interview Preparation
- [ ] 30- and 90-second introductions
- [ ] Knowledge of prospective employer's interview strategy
- [ ] Prepared questions for recruiter/HR manager/hiring manager
- [ ] Post-interview follow-up strategy

Networking with Purpose
☐ Apply the <u>Nine Ways to Networking with Purpose</u>

☐ Adopt framework for networking using <u>Advice/Information/Referral</u>

☐ Prepare conversation starters

☐ Develop a network contact strategy

Being Present in Your New Role
☐ Prepare your persona going forward

☐ Learn the history of the organization

☐ Develop a 30-, 60-, 90-day plan

☐ Build relationships

Final Exercise: Insights into Action

Insights into Action is one of the most important components of our leadership program. The intent is to use a 3-2-1 countdown method to encourage our people to take immediate action on at least one deed to create forward momentum. We encourage you to use this form to create similar momentum in your job search or career change.

What **3** insights have you gained from reading our book and doing the exercises at the end of select chapters? What **2** actions will you immediately commit to, such as updating your resume, adding confidants to your network, asking your employer to discuss your career, creating S.T.A.R. stories? Now, what **1** insight will you act on before your next job or career change?

Three insights I have gained

_____

_____

_____

Two actions, based on my insights, I am committed to apply

_____

_____

One action item I will act on before my next job or career move

_____

About the Authors

Michael P. Grubich

President & Managing Partner – LAK Group

As a President and Managing Partner at the LAK Group, Michael Grubich brings more than 25 years of global leadership experience that enhances the performance of the organizations, individuals, teams, and leaders that he serves.

Michael helps organizations think strategically regarding human capital in order to move from concepts to practical implementation in all areas, from selection to succession. He provides consultation and coaching to senior leaders in order to help them move their businesses forward through an integrated approach of aligning talent, culture, and business objectives.

Prior to joining LAK Group, Michael served in several global thought and operational leadership roles at Aurora Health Care, CNH Industrial, Kohler Company, Jockey International and Six Flags Theme Parks. During this time, he led a variety of global human resources functions, including Talent Management, Leadership Development, Talent Acquisition, Succession Management, Learning and Organizational Development, Assessment, Change Management, Strategic Planning, Diversity & Inclusion and Workforce Management Practices.

Michael holds a Bachelor of Science degree from Northern Illinois University and earned his Master's degree in Business Administration (MBA) from Lake Forest Graduate School of Business. Outside of work, Mike serves as Chairman, Board of Directors for Special Olympics in Wisconsin, and served as the Board Chair for Catholic Memorial High School in Waukesha, Wisconsin. He is also an adjunct faculty member at Marquette University's College of Business Administration and the University of Wisconsin-Milwaukee.

Michael can be reached at: mgrubich@lak-group.com

Mike Milsted

President & Managing Partner – LAK Group

As a President and Managing Partner at the LAK Group, Mike Milsted brings more than 25 years of experience working for Fortune 100 companies with global leadership responsibilities to working within small family-owned businesses on main street.

Mike strives to live his values, to create balance in his life, and to have a meaningful impact on others...On Purpose. He is driven by a passion to engage people and organizations in their purpose and to find meaningful involvement in all they do.

While he thrived on the competitive landscape of Corporate America, his calling to build something more meaningful, something he could truly believe in, was undeniable and so he took a leap of faith and embarked on a journey to create something truly special. Mike's goal has always been to create a meaningful impact on others, and to live his values. He is not afraid to take risks, and his nature allows him to simplify the complex.

At LAK Group, Mike has created an organization that shares his values and passion for empowering people and organizations to identify and live their passion with purpose. As a leader in the management consulting industry, he has helped employers address the changing demands of digital transformation, and serves as a trusted sounding board for clients to solve problems. Mike helps his customers balance and implement the ideals of leadership development and career development, talent management, and culture.

Mike understands the importance of balancing the needs of both organizations and individuals, and seeks to understand the unique challenges facing business leaders in today's fast-paced and ever-changing world. He specializes in areas such as strategy, talent management, leadership coaching, mentoring, change management, succession planning, retention, and assessment.

Mike got his start as a Social Worker at a local family advocacy shelter and is deeply committed to making a difference in his community through volunteer organizations like the Boy Scouts of America, National Kidney Foundation, and Habitat for Humanity.

Mike believes that we all have a responsibility to use our talents and resources to make the world a better place, and he is proud to be part of a company that shares that same belief.

Mike can be reached at: mmilsted@lak-group.com

About LAK Group

At the LAK Group, we work with leaders and individuals to discover their Human Capital Advantage. Our team of seasoned management consulting professionals has been in your shoes, so we understand the hurdles that you need to clear to get things done. That's why we create plans for culture, development, retention, and outplacement for a range of clients in a variety of industries.

To support individuals in their career growth, we have developed one of our signature programs, Career Fit™. The details of this program are listed below.

CareerFIT
POWERED BY THE LAK GROUP

A guided journey to get your CareerFIT™ to achieve Professional Fulfillment

Why CareerFIT:

- Plan the trajectory of your career by aligning with your natural strengths and interests
- Develop a road map for going forward
- Get answers to the tough questions, like:
  - Am I in the right place?
  - Am I doing the right thing?
  - Am I having the impact I want to have?

- Reveal what motivates you at work and how you arrived where you are now
- Highlight what uniquely sets you apart from others
- Capitalize on your natural strengths and identify the areas to work on to maximize success
- Understand what drives your best performance

Workshops	• Three, virtual, live workshops • Assessments, Discussions, and Exercises to assist you on your journey
1:1 Coaching	• Three individual coaching sessions • Personal discussions about what you are working on and how to give it more meaning
Group Coaching	• One group coaching session • Discussions and sharing to help participants learn from each other

CareerFIT™ offers an experience that is different

- A guided process by professional facilitators and coaches
- 1:1 coaching with career and executive coaches
- Research-backed strengths and career alignment assessments
- Collaborative environment with peers
- Network expansion and development of relationships that last for a lifetime

"If you don't know where you're going, any road will take you there."
-Lewis Carroll

Sign Up Now!

Visit our website at www.lakgroup.com

Follow us at www.linkedin.com/company/lakgroup/

LAK Group
375 Bishops Way, Suite 230
Brookfield, WI 53005 - (262) 786-9200

References

1. Pew Research Polling and Analysis (November 18, 2017). *Where Americans Find Meaning in Life*. Pew Research Center. Retrieved from https://www.pewforum.org/2018/11/20/where-americans-find-meaning-in-life/

2. Frankl, Viktor E. (June 1, 2006). *Man's Search for Meaning (Original edition out of print)*. Boston: Beacon Press. Retrieved from https://www.amazon.com/Mans-Search-Meaning-Viktor-Frankl/dp/080701429X

3. Alimujiang A, Wiensch A, Boss J, et al. (2019). *Association Between Life Purpose and Mortality Among US Adults Older Than 50 Years*. JAMA Network Open. 2(5):e194270. Retrieved from https://jamanetwork.com/journals/jamanetworkopen/fullarticle/2734064

4. Herzberg, Frederick (October 27, 2017). *Motivation to Work*. Oxfordshire: Routledge Publishing. Retrieved from https://www.amazon.com/Motivation-Work-Frederick-Herzberg-dp-1138536911/dp/1138536911/ref=mt_other?_encoding=UTF8&me=&qid=

5. Bureau of Labor Statistics (August 31, 2021). *Number of Jobs, Labor Market Experience, Marital Status, and Health: Results from a National Longitudinal Survey*. U.S. Department of Labor. Retrieved from https://www.bls.gov/news.release/pdf/nlsoy.pdf

6. Kelly, Jack (September 4, 2019). *Breadcrumbing: How to Read the Signs and Avoid Being Strung Along in Your Career*. Forbes. Retrieved from https://www.forbes.com/sites/jackkelly/2019/09/04/breadcrumbing-how-to-read-the-signs-and-avoid-being-strung-along-in-your-career/?sh=24405d474b6b

7. Statista (May, 2021). *Leading Banks in the U.S. 2020, by Number of Employees*. Retrieved from https://www.statista.com/statistics/250220/ranking-of-united-states-banks-by-number-of-employees-in-2012/

8. Hedge A. & Nou, D. (July 23, 2018). *Worker Reactions to Electro-chromatic and Low e Glass Office Windows*. Ergonomics International Journal. Vol 2, Issue 4. Retrieved from https://medwinpublishers.com/EOIJ/EOIJ16000166.pdf

9.   Melore, Chris (February 6, 2022). *Survey: 55% of High Schoolers Don't Think College Is Needed for a Successful Career.* Study Finds. Retrieved from https://www.studyfinds.org/high-school-students-college-career/

10.   Del Ray, Jason (December 11, 2019). *How Robots Are Transforming Amazon Warehouse Jobs — for Better and Worse.* Vox.com. Retrieved from https://www.vox.com/recode/2019/12/11/20982652/robots-amazon-warehouse-jobs-automation

11.   Weise, Karen (November 27, 2020). *Pushed by Pandemic, Amazon Goes on a Hiring Spree Without Equal.* The New York Times. Retrieved from https://www.nytimes.com/2020/11/27/technology/pushed-by-pandemic-amazon-goes-on-a-hiring-spree-without-equal.html

12.   United States Census Bureau (2017). *ACS 1-Year Estimates.* Retrieved from https://www.census.gov/programs-surveys/acs/technical-documentation/table-and-geography-changes/2017/1-year.html#par_textimage_0

13.   Rath, Tom & Harter, Jim. (May 4, 2010). *The Five Essential Elements of Well-Being.* Gallup Workplace. Retrieved from https://www.gallup.com/workplace/237020/five-essential-elements.aspx

14.   Saad, Lydia & Wigert, Ben (October 13, 2021). *Remote Work Persisting and Trending Permanent.* Gallup News. Retrieved from https://news.gallup.com/poll/355907/remote-work-persisting-trending-permanent.aspx

15.   Becker Friedman Institute (September 2, 2020). *Key Economic Findings About COVID-19.* University of Chicago. Retrieved from https://bfi.uchicago.edu/key-economic-facts-about-covid-19/

16.   Monticello Public School District. *Career Paths.* Retrieved from https://www.monticello.k12.mn.us/domain/625

17.   Gallup Analytics (2018). *How Does the Gallup-Sharecare Well-Being Index Work?* Gallup Research. Retrieved from https://www.gallup.com/175196/gallup-healthways-index-methodology.aspx

18. Rinne, April (August 24, 2021). *Flux, 8 Superpowers for Thriving in Constant Change*. San Francisco: Berrett Koehler, p 2. Retrieved from https://www.amazon.com/Flux-Superpowers-Thriving-Constant-Change/dp/1523093595/ref=sr_1_1?crid=2L88SQ7LPH2ST&keywords=April+rinne&qid=1643917429&sprefix=april+rinne%2Caps%2C462&sr=8-1

19. Ladders, Inc. (November 6, 2018). *"Ladders Updates Popular Recruiter Eye-Tracking Study With New Key Insights on How Job Seekers Can Improve Their Resumes."* Cision PR Newswire. Retrieved from https://www.prnewswire.com/news-releases/ladders-updates-popular-recruiter-eye-tracking-study-with-new-key-insights-on-how-job-seekers-can-improve-their-resumes-300744217.html

20. Peters, Tom (August 31, 1997). *The Brand Called You*. Fast Company. Retrieved from https://www.fastcompany.com/28905/brand-called-you

21. Sinek, Simon & Mead, David & Docker, Peter (September 5, 2017). *Find Your Why: A Practical Guide for Discovering Purpose for You and Your Team*. Portfolio Publishing. Retrieved from https://www.amazon.com/Find-Your-Why-Practical-Discovering/dp/0143111728/ref=sxin_10_mbs_w_global_sims?content-id=amzn1.sym.167d0880-9da0-400b-938e-4382731a4102%3Aamzn1.sym.167d0880-9da0-400b-938e-4382731a4102&crid=1WZBTRUM2DEUW&cv_ct_cx=simon+sinek+start+with+why+book&keywords=simon+sinek+start+with+why+book&pd_rd_i=0143111728&pd_rd_r=0bedb728-8e7c-4cfc-bb65-d602153f53ff&pd_rd_w=wkio2&pd_rd_wg=a0kcv&pf_rd_p=167d0880-9da0-400b-938e-4382731a4102&pf_rd_r=A00TER2VH2F1G9HJSJP-M&qid=1658415360&sprefix=simon+sinek%2Caps%2C54&sr=1-1-9e7645f9-2d19-4bff-863e-f6cdbe50f990

22. Khabab, Osama (January 15, 2020). *Four Steps to Crafting a Strong Brand Message*. Forbes. Retrieved from https://www.forbes.com/sites/forbesagencycouncil/2020/01/15/four-steps-to-crafting-a-strong-brand-message/?sh=2c5279553555

23. Boris, Vanessa (December 20, 2017). *What Makes Storytelling So Effective For Learning?* Harvard Business Publishing. Retrieved from https://www.harvardbusiness.org/what-makes-storytelling-so-effective-for-learning/

24. Wargo, Eric (July 1, 2006). *"How Many Seconds to a First Impression?"* Association for Psychological Science. Retrieved from https://www.psychologicalscience.org/observer/how-many-seconds-to-a-first-impression

25. Stahl, Ashley (November 6, 2015) *"How to Land a Job in 90 Seconds."* Forbes. Retrieved from https://www.forbes.com/sites/ashleystahl/2015/11/06/how-to-land-a-job-in-90-seconds/?sh=1aa7d89b4802

26. Thompson, Jeff (September 30, 2011). *"Is Nonverbal Communication a Numbers Game?"* Psychology Today. Retrieved from https://www.psychologytoday.com/us/blog/beyond-words/201109/is-nonverbal-communication-numbers-game

27. Jaser, Zahira & Petrakaki, Dimitra & Starr, Rachel & Oyarbide-Magaria, Ernesto (January 27, 2022). *Where Automated Job Interviews Fall Short.* Harvard Business Review. Retrieved from https://hbr.org/2022/01/where-automated-job-interviews-fall-short

28. Cao, Jiyin & Smith, Edward (October 1, 2021). *Why Are Some People More Reluctant to Network Than Others?* Kellogg Insight, Kellogg School of Management, Northwestern University. Retrieved from https://insight.kellogg.northwestern.edu/article/network-size-social-status

29. Adler, Lou (February 29, 2016). *New Survey Reveals 85% of All Jobs Are Filled Via Networking.* LinkedIn. Retrieved from https://www.linkedin.com/pulse/new-survey-reveals-85-all-jobs-filled-via-networking-lou-adler

30. Covey, Stephen R. (May 19, 2020) *The 7 Habits of Highly Effective People: 30th Anniversary Edition.* Simon & Schuster. p. 273. Retrieved from https://www.amazon.com/Habits-Highly-Effective-People-Powerful/dp/1982137274/ref=sr_1_1?keywords=the+seven+habits&qid=1664628243&qu=eyJxc2MiOiIyLjIzIiwicXNhIjoiMS42NyIsInFzcCI6IjEuOTTgifQ%3D%3D&sr=8-1&asin=1982137274&revisionId=&format=4&depth=1

31.   Grubich, Michael P. & Smith, Shelley A. (February 19, 2021) *Leadership ON PURPOSE: How Agile Leaders Inspire Others.* Independently Published. p 57. Retrieved from https://www.amazon.com/ Leadership-PURPOSE-Leaders-Inspire-Others/dp/B08WZCVC18/ ref=sr_1_1?crid=3FQMBTBXTFPGE&keywords=leadership+on+purpose&qid=1665237255&qu=eyJxc2MiOiIwLjAwIiwicXNhIjoiMC4wMCIsInFzcCI6IjAuMDAifQ%3D%3D&sprefix=leadership+on+purpose%2Caps%2C144&sr=8-1&asin=B08WZCVC18&revisionId=&format=4&depth=1

32.   Grubich, Michael P. & Smith, Shelley A. (February 19, 2021). *Leadership ON PURPOSE: How Agile Leaders Inspire Others.* p. 131. Retrieved from https://www.amazon.com/Leadership-PURPOSE-Leaders-Inspire-Others/dp/B08WZCVC18/ref=tmm_pap_swatch_0?_encoding=UTF8&qid=1670436835&sr=8-1&asin=B08WZCVC18&revisionId=&format=4&depth=1

33.   Mcleod, Saul, PhD (April 4, 2022). *Maslow's Hierarchy of Needs. Simple Psychology.* Retrieved from https://www.simplypsychology.org/maslow.html

34.   Nickerson, Charlotte (November 16, 2021). *Herzberg's Motivation Two-Factor Theory.* Simply Psychology. Retrieved from www.simplypsychology.org/herzbergs-two-factor-theory.html

35.   ibid

36.   Grubich, Michael P. & Smith, Shelley A. (February 19, 2021). *Leadership ON PURPOSE: How Agile Leaders Inspire Others.* p. 104. Retrieved from https://www.amazon.com/Leadership-PURPOSE-Leaders-Inspire-Others/dp/B08WZCVC18/ref=tmm_pap_swatch_0?_encoding=UTF8&qid=1670436835&sr=8-1&asin=B08WZCVC18&revisionId=&format=4&depth=1

37.   Hartley, Deanna (November 14, 2016). *73% of Employers Would Negotiate Salary, 55% of Workers Don't Ask.* Career Builder. Retrieved from https:// resources.careerbuilder.com/news-research/73-of-employers-would-negotiate-salary-55-of-workers-don-t-ask

38. Fidelity Investments (May 4, 2022). *2022 Career Assessment Study* [Press Release]. Retrieved from https://newsroom.fidelity.com/press-releases/news-details/2022/Fidelity-Study-Shows-Young-Professionals-on-the-Move-Six-in-Ten-Have-Changed-Jobs-During-the-Pandemic-or-Expect-to-Be-at-a-Different-Company-Within-Two-Years/default.aspx

39. Kaiser Family Foundation (November 10, 2021). *2021 Employer Health Benefits Survey*. Retrieved from https://www.kff.org/report-section/ehbs-2021-summary-of-findings/

40. Grubich, Michael P. & Smith, Shelley A. (February 19, 2021). *Leadership ON PURPOSE: How Agile Leaders Inspire Others*. p. 51. Retrieved from https://www.amazon.com/Leadership-PURPOSE-Leaders-Inspire-Others/dp/B08WZCVC18/ref=tmm_pap_swatch_0?_encoding=UTF8&qid=1670436835&sr=8-1&asin=B08WZCVC18&revisionId=&format=4&depth=1

41. Covey, Stephen R. (November 9, 2004). *The 7 Habits of Highly Effective People: Powerful Lessons in Personal Change*. Free Press. p 235. Retrieved from https://www.amazon.com/Habits-Highly-Effective-People-Powerful/dp/0743269519/ref=sr_1_8?crid=3567XY0DEZOH7&keywords=7+Habits+of+Highly+Effective+People&qid=1675973523&sprefix=7+habits+of+highly+effective+people%2Caps%2C199&sr=8-8

42. Watkins, Michael D. (May 14 2013). *The First 90 Days: Proven Strategies for Getting Up to Speed Faster and Smarter*. Harvard Business Review Press. Updated, expanded edition, p2. Retrieved from https://www.amazon.com/First-90-Days-Strategies-Expanded/dp/1422188612/ref=asc_df_1422188612/?tag=hyprod-20&linkCode=df0&hvadid=266118767273&hvpos=&hvnetw=g&hvrand=4788696057254664775&hvpone=&hvptwo=&hvqmt=&hvdev=c&hvdvcmdl=&hvlocint=&hvlocphy=9010805&hvtargid=pla-404766147599&psc=1&region_id=972485&asin=1422188612&revisionId=&format=4&depth=1

43. Covey, Stephen R. (November 9, 2004). *The 7 Habits of Highly Effective People: Powerful Lessons in Personal Change*. Free Press. p 150. Retrieved from https://www.amazon.com/Habits-Highly-Effective-People-Powerful/dp/0743269519/ref=sr_1_8?crid=3567XY0DEZOH7&keywords=7+Habits+of+Highly+Effective+People&qid=1675973523&sprefix=7+habits+of+highly+effective+people%2Caps%2C199&sr=8-8

44. Bauer, Talya N. (2010), *Onboarding New Employees. Maximizing Success*. SHRM Foundation's Effective Practice Guide Series. SHRM Foundation. Retrieved from https://www.shrm.org/foundation/ourwork/initiatives/resources-from-past-initiatives/Documents/Onboarding%20New%20Employees.pdf?utm_source=link_wwwv9&utm_campaign=item_235121&utm_medium=copy

45. Oosterhof, N. N., & Todorov, A. (2008). *The Functional Basis of Face Evaluation*. Proceedings of the National Academy of Sciences, 105 (32), 11087-11092. Retrieved from https://www.pnas.org/doi/abs/10.1073/pnas.0805664105

46. Grubich, Michael P. & Smith, Shelley A. (February 19, 2021). *Leadership ON PURPOSE: How Agile Leaders Inspire Others*. p. 19. Retrieved from https://www.amazon.com/Leadership-PURPOSE-Leaders-Inspire-Others/dp/B08WZCVC18/ref=tmm_pap_swatch_0?_encoding=UTF8&qid=1670436835&sr=8-1&asin=B08WZCVC18&revisionId=&format=4&depth=1

Made in United States
Orlando, FL
15 December 2023

40974624R00127